When Worry Works

When Worry Works

How to Harness Your Parenting Stress and Guide Your Teen to Success

Dana Dorfman, PhD

ROWMAN & LITTLEFIELD
Lanham • Boulder • New York • London

Published by Rowman & Littlefield
An imprint of The Rowman & Littlefield Publishing Group, Inc.
4501 Forbes Boulevard, Suite 200, Lanham, Maryland 20706
www.rowman.com

86-90 Paul Street, London EC2A 4NE

British Library Cataloguing in Publication Information Available

Library of Congress Cataloging-in-Publication Data

Names: Dorfman, Dana, author.
　Title: When worry works : how to harness your parenting stress and guide
　　your teen to success / Dana Dorfman.
　Description: Lanham : Rowman & Littlefield, [2023] | Includes
　　bibliographical references and index.
　Identifiers: LCCN 2022039390 (print) | LCCN 2022039391 (ebook) | ISBN
　　9781538164532 (cloth ; alk. paper) | ISBN 9781538164549 (ebook)
　Subjects: LCSH: Parent and teenager. | Parenting--Psychological aspects. |
　　Anxiety.
　Classification: LCC HQ799.15 .D67 2023　(print) | LCC HQ799.15　(ebook) |
　　DDC 649/.125--dc23/eng/20220915
　LC record available at https://lccn.loc.gov/2022039390
　LC ebook record available at https://lccn.loc.gov/2022039391

To Scott—as we continue to grow, together
To Ava and Eli—your true selves

Contents

Acknowledgments

Book writing, like raising children, takes a village of guides, mentors, and role models. Words can barely capture the depth of gratitude I have for the villagers—the many friends, family, colleagues, office mates, and supervisors—who generously supported this project through conversation, connections, advice, and expertise. And though it's difficult to capture every person by name, please know how appreciative I am for your contributions.

Knowing that succinctness is not my forte, I've attempted to consolidate the list:

Thank you to my many dear friends, whose humor, positivity, and acceptance sustain me—Jenny Theriault and Debbie Evans (and the unfortunate restaurant waiters who endured our hours of deep analyses); the Fab 5, for forty years of laughter and love; and to many walks and talks, coffees, and hours of listening with Erin Tashian, Lisa Usdan, Ellen Jacobs, Jenny Zaslow, and my podcast co-host (the other Mom on the Couch), Amy Veltman. By opening your hearts and minds, you have enhanced mine tenfold.

Thank you to Mya Dunlop and the Teen Brain Trust Team for your ongoing collaboration and shared passion to improve teen mental health through awareness and compassion. Robin Friend Stift—I can't thank you enough for masterfully synthesizing hundreds of pages into refined and focused chapters. Thank you to Annie Schoening, who can make content from anything that I say, tolerating my resistance to social media and maintaining patience while helping me to discover a values-aligned way to participate.

And a heartfelt shout-out to Holly Ojalvo, who swooped in, managed, and assuaged my paralyzing deadline anxiety.

Thank you, Jeffrey Davis, and the Tracking Wonder team (particularly Britt Bravo), for not only mentoring me through the writing process but for guiding me "back to" my own spirit and reintroducing me to my "young genius." Together, we identified and harnessed my values, so this book progressed with intention and purpose.

Thank you to my agent, Jennifer Unter, for our fortuitous reconnection, your expertise and reassurance, and for believing in this project and helping me to navigate the publishing process. And to my editor, Suzanne Staszak-Silva from Rowman & Littlefield, thank you for taking a chance on a first-time author, for your valuable edits, and for imparting your extensive publishing knowledge.

To my FOO (family of origin): Mom and Dad, for modeling the parenting life cycle with grace and honesty—thank you for instilling the value of achievement in me and for inspiring me to continue growing, to embrace change, and to evolve throughout parenthood. To my brothers, Rick and Craig, thank you for sharing your humor, wisdom, and contacts, in support of my professional and personal advancement. You both mean so much to me.

Words cannot capture the depth of gratitude to my current family; we four (plus Winnie) are miraculous. Scott, for our indescribable quarter-century-plus partnership; for your endless support, encouragement, belief, and true appreciation for every symbolic level of this process. Thank you for trusting my theories and perspectives to create and raise the two most empathic, perceptive, wise, engaging, self-aware teens I know! I hope that we continue to validate, cherish, and encourage their true selves to grow so that they may continue to lead lives with intention, self-defined meaning, and fulfillment.

Thank you, Ava, for your hours of deep analysis, challenging yourself and valuing your beautiful evolution, and embracing the importance of being a "good person" even when your world's primary focus was on achievement! And thank you, Eli, for your courageous examination and masterful expression of your heart and mind; your strength of character never ceases to amaze me. I would like to promise both of you that I will no longer mention "the book," but . . .

And of course, to the many families, the parents and teens who have entrusted me with their stories, vulnerability, and emotions. My deepest wish is that I've offered the emotional safety for you to explore, discover, and express your lives in alignment with your authentic selves.

Introduction

Any parent of our generation knows *that* parent—the one many of us secretly fear we could become if we let our worries (love?) get the best of us—that seemingly unhinged parent who has few qualms about calling a teacher to complain about her teen's grade, or the one who secretly writes (edits?) his teen's essay because the stakes for this grade are so high that they could make or break the GPA, or the one who stands on the sidelines of the field yelling at the ref and privately ranks players' progress to ensure their teens' good standing. The helicopter, the snowplow, the tiger—you are not one of those! And you are *definitely* not the celebrity or billionaire parent who paid off a sociopathic college counselor to get their high school senior into a "highly selective" college, that parent who is essentially one or two or three iterations of achievement fanaticism more than you are, or could ever be.

Can you believe the nerve? Have they no moral compass? The entitlement!

Am I presumptuous to suspect that you are a deeply loving and devoted parent who takes your role seriously? You're the parent who believes in helping your teen "live their best life" and achieve their potential. You read about parenting, you attend school meetings and seminars, you talk to other parents, and you find yourself thinking a lot about your teen's future, hoping that they'll be equipped to lead happy and fulfilling lives.

You know you're not *that* parent. Nonetheless, even though you don't like the hypercompetitive system, you're all too aware of the realities your teens face. You're trying to figure out the sweet spot to promote

your teen's success . . . happily. You want to feel like you've done right
by them and held up your end of the successful parenting bargain.

And you also worry about the pressure. You cannot avoid the statistics reflecting the staggering increase in adolescent mental health
crises—anxiety, depression, and suicide rates are higher than they have
ever been in our nation's history.

It's terrifying.

I get it. I'm the mom of two teens. I marvel and enjoy. I worry and
fret. I secretly judge others and compare (although now the secret's
out!). I love them and feel desperate to do parenting right. And yes,
many days I fall short. I focus more on checking off my daily to-do
list, or merely getting through the day, which means I lose sight of my
values, myself, and them.

My husband and I struggle with achievement-related dilemmas, big
and small—the value of travel leagues, quitting instrument lessons,
investing in enrichment classes, and dilemmas about academic rigor
and our kids' academic performance. We often ask ourselves, "Are we
doing enough to help them be successful?"

This is the problem that most parents are grappling with—how to
help our kids be successful—to become happy, healthy, functioning
adults who live fulfilling and satisfying lives in the midst of our increasingly pressured world.

I've devoted my thirty-year psychotherapy career to understanding
how adolescents thrive and how their parents and the people who love
them can foster this flourishing. In my office, I witness the up-close-
and-personals of adolescents' inner lives, and I sit with parents who
expose their behind-the-scenes fears about the suffocating pressures.
They *and* we are exhaustively challenged to keep up with the accelerat-
ing pace and intensity of the modern world.

And while we yearn for a change, many of us feel too overwhelmed
and powerless to do anything about it. Even if the systems conflict with
our principles, we know "it's the way things are," and we have accepted
that we must play along. Since we can't change the educational systems, solve the world's problems, and influence college competition,
we begrudgingly continue doing what we've been doing—keeping up,
absorbing the pressure, and trying to prevent ourselves and our kids
from falling apart.

Here's the thing: When we feel and think like this, we inadvertently perpetuate the problem. What I've seen and personally experienced as a parent is that when we are unknowingly consumed by our own anxiety, we think, react, and act upon it. Anxiety prevents us from making decisions in accordance with our fundamental values, and it impedes our ability to support our teens in the ways that we intend. In our efforts to guide them, we unwittingly promote the paradoxical effect—stressed, depressed, and anxious teens. The research repeatedly confirms that parental stress negatively impacts teens. The more worried and stressed parents are, the more they engender or exacerbate teen stress. Many of us are engaging in what I call an achievement-anxiety feedback loop.

Here's the good news: While we may feel powerless to change the educational complex and we cannot *control* our teens, we *can* and *do* have the ability to shift and change our approach to both. And the starting block lies within us.

What I've experienced as a parent, and what I've seen in my work with hundreds of parents, is that by taking several self-reflective steps, we are able to shift our parenting approach, which then leads to improved mental health, greater clarity, and better relationships with our teens. And fortunately, this awareness doesn't require a deep dive—just some time, reflection, examination, and awareness of our innate *achievement anxiety.* By doing so, parents can manage and direct it in effective ways. These insights equip parents with more confidence, leading to less conflict, and less worry. When we harness our anxiety, we guide our teens toward authentic success.

We've all seen and read books on helping your teen with anxiety or managing academic stress, but this book offers parents a roadmap to recognize the ways that they may be inadvertently perpetuating or exacerbating their teens' stress. It equips parents with processes and tools to manage and harness their own anxieties, particularly when making achievement-related decisions, so that they can guide their teens toward success with the authenticity, values, and effectiveness they are seeking.

Part I lays the groundwork. In Chapter 1, we'll review the parenting landscape—the backdrop of our parenting worries, our cultural relationship with achievement, and how and why it can become the center of our parenting focus. This chapter will introduce you to the concept of parental achievement anxiety.

Chapter 2 will review the inner workings of anxiety, clarifying its definition, purpose, and influence on our daily functioning. This chapter will remind you not only of anxiety's limitations, but its benefits, making what is unconscious more conscious. Through case examples, the chapter highlights how anxiety affects parents' mind-sets and behaviors.

Chapter 3 explains and illustrates anxiety's impact on our thinking—specifically, worries. The chapter identifies some common anxious thinking patterns/thought distortions (worries) and offers examples of how parents react to them. Your knowledge of these thought patterns will help cue you that anxiety is present.

Each one of these chapters will reinforce the importance of familiarizing yourself with your own anxiety patterns so that you may have more control over how you use them to your advantage—making your worries work *for* you, rather than against you.

In Part II, chapters 4 through 11 will further your understanding of the role parents' anxieties play in the achievement-anxiety spiral. Drawn from a compilation of parents and teens that I've treated, you will be offered an up-close look at how parent achievement anxiety plays out in families. Through the descriptions and case examples of eight different archetypes—Parent Anxiety Reaction Types (PARTs)—you'll gain a deeper and more nuanced understanding of the ways that parent anxiety manifests, and recognize how you can work through it to more effectively respond to your teens.

Each chapter illustrates the triggers, thought patterns, and perks and pitfalls of each reaction type, and the ways that your awareness of your anxiety can help you to improve your relationship with your teens. Understanding your particular anxiety can equip you to parent in accordance with your values, rather than merely reacting to your anxieties. By doing so, you will improve your well-being and your relationship with your teens, becoming better equipped to confidently guide your teens toward authentic success.

In Part III, Chapter 12 brings it all together, assisting you in clarifying your values. In order to make decisions which "feel right," we need to know what our own deep-seated beliefs are. This clarification and identification process enables you to reflect on how you want to live your life, what you want to instill in your teens, and what can serve as your North Star or reliable anchors when you are feeling anxious and adrift.

The appendix offers a decision-making worksheet which will guide you through the process of integrating your values and your anxieties as you work to solve your parenting dilemmas.

So pause, take a deep breath, and let's take this journey—together.

PART I

Why, What, and How
Parents Worry

Chapter 1

The Dilemma du Jour

"When society becomes too focused on narrow definitions of success (like grades, test scores, prestige, and performance), kids have less space to develop the skills they need to become resilient and engaged learners and to grow into healthy young adults."

—Challenge Success

MENTAL HEALTH MAKES THE HEADLINES

If there were ever a time that mental health should be given its due attention, it's now. Finally, the cat's out of the bag. In daily headlines and news stories, on social media[1] feeds from professional athletes to company employees, there is a growing national acknowledgment and acceptance of the idea that every human being has emotions, and that mental health challenges are universal.

There is not a segment of the population whose emotional well-being hasn't been impacted by the stress and challenges of the global pandemic. This international crisis has brought mental health to the forefront of our education systems, corporate environments, and of course, our dinner tables.

Bubbling to the surface of this global conversation is the mental health of teens and adolescents. Rates of teen anxiety, depression, and suicide have been rising steadily for decades,[2] and the global mental health crisis caused by the pandemic has only exacerbated the issue.[3]

Add to this anxiety over the climate,[4] worries about shootings and school safety,[5] the mental health hazards of social media, political unrest[6] and racial tension, and the mental health outlook for today's teens and adolescents is increasingly bleak.

The silver lining is that such an unavoidably worsening crisis has prompted mental health destigmatization movements, policy changes, and more accessible programs. This conveys and reinforces the critical message that *every* teen struggles with emotions, and that social-emotional health is as central to overall well-being as physical health.

Teens and adults today are seeking mental health consultation or treatment more than they have at any other time in our nation's history, which has led to a new problem: There are not enough programs and professionals to meet the outsized demand. My colleagues and I have extended waiting lists and are stretched to exhaustion trying to meet the needs of our communities. And burnt-out therapists are something that our country cannot afford.

We are all caretakers of our own mental health. As parents we get double duty, caring for ourselves as well as our kids. Any good flight attendant will tell you, in an emergency, you need to put on your own oxygen mask before helping your kid with theirs. We can't help our kids if we are incapacitated. When it comes to mental health and managing our anxieties, that guideline is more important than ever.

MY CRISIS DU JOUR

As I write this, I'm in the throes of a parenting anxiety spiral. Three days ago, I would have said that both of my teens were "okay." They've adjusted to their respective semesters, seem to be learning a lot, appear to be relatively content, have nice groups of friends, and are experiencing the preliminary freedoms of lifted mask mandates and reduced viral spread (compared to the past two years, at least). As I was on the verge of cautiously exhaling, *bam*, the crisis du jour arose.

While attending a Super Bowl party (Rams vs. Bengals) at my son's best friend's home, several of the other parents were discussing their sons' plans for next fall. Assuming that I had already heard, they described application and interview processes and the boys' hopeful acceptances to European study abroad programs for next year (their junior year of high school).

"Back up a minute," I said. "Is that for *this* coming fall semester?" This was the first I'd heard of any of this.

As they elaborated, I slowly began to put the pieces together. Three out of four of my son's tight-knit group of friends were venturing into language immersion programs in Spain and France next semester. My son was the only one remaining at home.

Wait—what? I thought. I'd never even heard of these programs. was this some new pre-college thing—something else I didn't know about? Our daughter was currently studying abroad as a *college* junior, but high school? Had we missed the boat, literally and figuratively?

As they proceeded to describe the program's offerings and their mixed feelings about the prospect of their sixteen-year-old leaving home for a year, I could not mask my own worries. Ironically, just hours before this party, I'd been seated at my computer writing this book about the perils of parental anxiety. And now, my own had been ignited! As they continued to chomp on their chicken wings and sip their beer, I tried to manage the growing pit in my stomach.

Under usual circumstances, I know that I would have been less jarred. However, my son's high school experience had already been massively fragmented by the pandemic. Adolescence was challenging enough without the daily unpredictability of hybrid schooling, ever-changing COVID protocols, and chronic health risks.

Along with every other parent in the country, I had been increasingly worried about the pandemic's impact on my teen's development, emotionally, socially, and academically. I was yearning for him to have some semblance of continuity and normalcy, and anticipating a very welcome "close-to-normal" year.

Every high school parent knows that junior year is the most stressful and meaningful of all four years of high school, the one that *really* counts. The time when college stress amps up, complete with college tours, standardized tests, and conversations about the future. I had steadied myself with the knowledge that my son had the support, stability, and loyalty of these three friends; they were "his people."

Despite the stress of the pandemic, this group of four had developed a uniquely special bond. Through their banter, virtual video gaming, hours of FaceTime, and long, masked walks all over Brooklyn, they'd become a social-emotional life raft for one another. They've supported each other through family losses, divorcing parents, romantic breakups, and the repeated disappointments of canceled activities, frustrations, and uncertainties of the pandemic. I had found great solace and gratitude in knowing they have each other to rely on. His friends' parents shared similar sentiments. "Knowing that they have one another has made the pandemic so much more bearable, for them and for me. It is a true friendship," one mom said to me.

As a practicing psychotherapist, I have devoted my entire thirty-year career to adolescent mental health, treating teens and their parents, writing, researching, and speaking on the topic. And while I've always had a rich appreciation for the stresses of adolescents and their parents, the crises of the past several years have led me, and every other parent, to pay special attention to my teen's well-being. We are all reading the tea leaves of our teens' behaviors to try to assess if they're okay. By the very nature of my work, I witness many instances and daily examples of when and how they are not.

So, when I watch this group of friends interact and overhear their conversations, I secretly exhale, relieved that they have one another. Of course, from a clinical perspective, I am well aware of how fundamentally important peer relationships are during this life stage. As teens emotionally separate from their parents and forge their own identities, they need to prioritize and deepen friendships, find safe people in whom they can confide, and experience a sense of belonging. These friendships are essential to healthy emotional development.

Until reaching this point in parenting, my husband and I had prided ourselves on not becoming involved in our teens' social dynamics (and I have advised many other parents to do the same). We are strong believers in our kids managing their own relationships, and that, through experience, they will learn the ins and outs of friendship. The best way for us to support them was from the sidelines. Now, suddenly, I find myself not only focusing on but obsessing about my son's social life!

Certainly, this is far from the greatest parenting challenge we've faced, and far from the worst thing that can happen to any adolescent. Objectively I *know* this will probably be a developmental growing pain or a blip on his teenage screen. But what if it's not? Just as I know how important close friendships are to teen survival, I also know how devastating the loss of them can be. And it's not just one friend; it's all three, at once—his closest confidants!

For the past several days, as I've felt myself entering this parenting anxiety spiral, I've been unable to talk myself out of it; it has consumed my thoughts. Unable to sleep, I lie awake at night, feeling sad on his behalf, imagining and fearing all that *could* happen, and devising ways that I might preempt his pain.

My worrying is not working well.

STRESSORS OF RAISING TODAY'S TEENS

Parenting teenagers has always been a notoriously dreaded time of parenting. It's viewed as a period of rebelliousness, sex, and drugs, not to mention college preparation and applications. However, parenting has never been as complicated as it is now, for many reasons. Parents are forced to contend with issues that didn't exist even a decade ago, and this quickly changing landscape offers us few personal comparison points to reference or to use as guidance. As parents try to stay on top of the world in which they're raising their teens, as well as get ahead of it to prepare them for their future, they cannot update as quickly as advancing technology and its corresponding societal changes.

The previous generation's appropriate (and not to be minimized) worries about teens' smoking, drinking, and dyeing their hair have transformed into worries about sexting, cyberbullying, TikTok, vaping, opioid addiction, school shootings, and a global pandemic.

In addition to being the most highly educated generation of parents,[7] we are also the most anxious. Inundated with parenting books and experts, we yearn for guidance and control. And with good reason. In addition to rising rates of anxiety, depression, and suicide in teens, we know our kids are facing an ever more uncertain economic future. Most parents of teens belong to Generation X, infamous as the first generation to have a lower quality of life (economically) than their parents. We fear a future in which our teens will struggle, and we feel compelled to give them every advantage, lest what happened to us happens to them.

In the face of these worries about the future, many parents come to the very logical conclusion that they must go the extra mile to ensure their kids' future success. So, we seek tangible ways to prepare our kids for the future and set them on a good path. Simply loving our teens doesn't seem like enough. Love won't pay their bills when they're older; we must ensure excellence in other areas.

This is why, in the back of my mind, as I toss and turn, worrying about my son's social life in his junior year of high school, my mind also wanders to how this will affect his college prospects. If his three best friends are all studying abroad in Europe, shouldn't he be doing the same? Will he be totally left behind? Will they be more likely to be accepted into their first-pick schools because of that experience, while my son's college application will look bland and unexciting in comparison? Should we enroll him in a study abroad program now? Is it too late?

I gently tap my husband's shoulder, requesting a reality check.

Patiently, he jokes, "Aren't you writing a book about this?"

Even though I've spent the better part of my career training myself to think differently, it's telling that in these moments of worry, my thoughts stray away from how this will affect my son's emotional and mental health to how it will affect his academic and career prospects. This is, after all, the default way most of us channel our anxieties. We want to *do* something with our anxious energy. We want to do something helpful, tangible, and practical. Something that will show results!

As important as mental and emotional health is, it's unhelpfully ephemeral. Too many variables go into it for us to be able to track it in a comfortably reliable way. So instead, we focus on more concrete metrics of success (like grades, test scores, sports, and other extracurricular achievements). For us parents, the easiest and most tangible part of our kids' lives to focus on is academic success.

PARENT ACHIEVEMENT ANXIETY

The first of the baby-boomer generation entered college in 1965. This marked a significant pivot in college admissions, from the old aristocracy (caste and connections) to the new "meritocracy" (scores and grades).[8] This was the origin of the system that exists today. The only thing that has changed since then is that it's gotten inexorably more competitive. There are higher expectations, slimmer acceptances, and more pressure on students. By the early 1980s, our nation's elite were learning to "game the system" with test prep and private college counseling. "College mania" has intensified and worsened every decade since.[9] What was once an opportunity has become a necessity, which means that modern parents are living in a world where economic uncertainty is on the rise and academic success has become increasingly competitive. This combination of factors triggers our anxiety (consciously or not), which makes us worry, and we channel our worries about the future into actions that will help our teens meet the benchmarks needed to succeed. Meanwhile, the bar for what our kids need to do to remain competitive in the future job market keeps getting higher and higher. We're in a perfect storm.

And the cost for our teens has been much too high.

- Emotional well-being on college campuses has fallen to the lowest level in its twenty-five-year history of being recorded.[10]
- In 2021, half of the college students reported feelings of hopelessness, and one-third said they were "so depressed it was difficult to function."[11]
- In a Harvard Graduate School of Education survey of 10,000 middle and high school students from diverse communities around the country, more than 50 percent ranked "achieving at a high level" as being more important than "happiness" or "caring for others."[12]
- Students from high-achieving schools face a higher probability of experiencing stress-related problems than students from other schools.[13]
- A 2018 Robert Wood Johnson Foundation study warned that "the excessive pressure to excel" had become a significant risk factor for the mental health of students in "high-achieving schools."[14]
- Preteens and teens from affluent, well-educated families (who are more likely to face family pressure to excel academically) experience among the highest rates of depression, substance abuse, anxiety disorders, somatic (bodily/physical) complaints, and unhappiness among any group of children in this country.[15]
- Suniya Luthar and Bronwyn Becker at Columbia University have found that kids whose parents overemphasize their achievements are more likely to have high levels of depression, anxiety, and substance abuse compared to other kids.[16]

You get the idea.

And if that wasn't bad enough, the idea that academic success leads to financial and career success is being categorically debunked. Several studies have shown that the greatest indicators of future success are emotional intelligence, along with the ability to empathize, problem-solve, self-regulate, manage stress, and communicate. These are backed up by findings from the Nobel Prize–winning economist, James Heckman, who posits, based on thirty-five years' worth of data, that character makes more of a difference than IQ for economic and social success.[17]

But I digress.

There's a direct correlation between the rise in achievement culture and the increase in teen anxiety and depression. Many of us know this already; I certainly do. And yet, as I lie awake at night worrying about my son, my thoughts inevitably drift toward how this new crisis will affect his academic performance. It's so automatic that it takes my husband's reminder that I'm writing a book about the perils of achievement anxiety for me to realize that this is exactly what I'm doing!

Luckily, he's right. I have the knowledge and tools necessary to redirect my worries in more positive directions. I know how important it is for me to manage my own anxiety and worries. The trap that so many parents fall into is when they feel anxious for their kids, they share those anxieties with them. It would be so easy for me to mention to my son that he should consider studying abroad or to confront him for not telling me his friends were applying to these programs. But both approaches would only add to the stress and pressure he is no doubt already feeling. I have spent years researching and working with parental stress. Study after study reveals that the way parents manage their stress is a primary indicator of their teens' well-being.[18] I must deal with my anxiety and worries in such a way that I don't transfer them on to my son.

So, I give myself the pep talk I would give a friend: "Validate *his* feelings when he decides to talk to you about what he's dealing with. Don't project *your* sadness onto him. Don't ask too many questions. Do not bring it up with him until he tells you about it. This is a growth opportunity; it doesn't have to be a harmful experience for him. Also, make sure to focus on his social and emotional health and not how this will affect his schoolwork or college prospects."

I experience a range of parental anxieties every day, and I'm always tempted to channel them in what I've learned is the most socially acceptable way: achievement. Yet, my daily interface with teen patients and their parents reminds me of the toxic effects of the well-intended, yet misguided, challenge of believing that anxiety translates into achievement. I'm trying to strike a balance. I want to prevent myself from falling into patterns where I give in to societal pressure and prioritize educational status over my son's well-being. At the same time, I still want to promote ambition and aspiration in my son.

So, I use the tried-and-true methods I share in this book to keep my parenting worries in check and ensure that my efforts to cultivate achievement in my son are driven by my values, not by my anxiety (or societal pressure). Like anything worth doing, it's a never-ending process and practice.

The takeaway for my fellow parents reading this is not that we *shouldn't* be focused on helping our teens to achieve academic and extracurricular success. Rather, it's that as a society, we have unconsciously adapted the habit of channeling our anxious thoughts into our drive to succeed. To truly help our teens succeed, we must learn to manage these anxieties so that we can define success and encourage achievement in accordance with our values. Otherwise, we perpetuate a culture where our anxiety drives achievement; eventually, we're too busy focusing on achievement to manage and deal with our anxiety.

The result? Our kids become like Sisyphus, eternally pushing a boulder up a never-ending hill.

Chapter 2

Anxiety Is the New Sugar

"There is nothing either good or bad but thinking makes it so."

—*Shakespeare*[1]

Like many women of my generation, I have spent the better part of my adulthood "watching my weight," prone to every diet and exercise fad that promises a slimmer waistline. I've gone through phases of cutting calories and eliminating entire food groups, and have done my fair share of fat-free and low-carb snacking. (SnackWell's cookies, anyone?) Unsurprisingly, the fads I've followed have not offered the long- or short-term results I was seeking. And the rest of the country hasn't benefited from weight-loss fads either. Obesity is still on the rise, heart disease is rampant, and there's an expanding prevalence of eating disorders. Ironically, our obsession with weight-loss trends has resulted in even worse health outcomes.

Then, in 2009, endocrinologist Robert Lustig[2] shared groundbreaking research identifying sugar as the hidden primary culprit responsible for many of the nation's weight and health problems. No longer just the cause of cavities and hyperactivity, the biological impact of sugar was far worse than we realized. One of the major problems with sugar was its insidious pervasiveness. It's in everything, not just cookies, cakes, and sodas. Unknowingly, we've been consuming sugar, or its many manufactured derivatives, in unexpected foods like tomato sauce and milk. This highly addictive hidden substance impacts every level of our functioning; it affects our energy, mood, appetite, and even our ability to think. But the tricky thing about sugar is that we can't just cut it out of our diet. We need it to survive.

Not all sugars are bad. In the right amounts, it can actually be very good, a useful tool when we're running low on energy. It's sugar's pervasiveness, the fact that it's in everything we eat, that's causing so many problems. But if we're aware of the sugar content in all our foods, we can be more discerning about our consumption and get the benefits of sugar without the major health disadvantages.

The same is true for anxiety. Like sugar, anxiety is much more pervasive than we realize. It can be found lurking in nearly every aspect of our lives. Every worried thought, self-protective impulse, and burst of adrenaline indicates that anxiety is present. But, like sugar, anxiety exists in many unexpected places. It's in the gym with us when we train, in the plans we make, in the affection we show, and is responsible for most, if not all, of our successes in life.

ANXIETY SHAMING

Anxiety, fear, and worry are all terms that have a bad rap. These aren't revered attributes or sought-after traits in our society. These words have all come to have negative connotations. Culturally, we associate them with weakness. They're uncomfortable and uncontrollable feelings that showcase our vulnerabilities. If you've got anxiety there must be something wrong with you, and in fact, you should probably be seeing a therapist.

Even though conversations destigmatizing anxiety and therapy are on the rise, many of us still associate these terms with character flaws and clinical diagnoses. We don't want to admit that we have anxieties, fears, or worries, even to ourselves, because that would be the same as admitting that we're weak or that we can't handle the challenges life has thrown at us.

Here's the simple truth: We all have anxiety. Especially me.

But seriously, anxiety is just a part of the human operating system. Having anxiety doesn't make us weak; it makes us human. And beyond that, anxiety, fear, and worry are all valuable tools that, when harnessed properly, can help us live richer and fuller lives. We can't get rid of these traits, but we can learn to direct their energies in more positive and productive ways. The first step toward doing so is accepting that we have anxiety. The second is learning how to recognize the ways it influences our behavior.

ANXIETY'S SWEET SPOT

At a track meet, as our teen paces before kneeling at the starting block, shaking out their feet and breathing heavily, we know that the anxiety they're feeling is beneficial. It will help them focus, fuel their legs, get them more oxygen, and run faster! Good! When college applications are coming up and our teen's anxiety prompts them to create and adhere to a writing schedule that will ensure their college essay gets done on time, that's great!

And we personally experience the beneficial effects of anxiety. Anxiety helps us prepare ahead of time for that upcoming trip to see our in-laws, and motivates us to knock off the recently gained holiday weight before our high-school reunion. Just the right amount of anxiety works beautifully for us; it's performance-enhancing.

Anxiety is actually an evolutionary advantage, rooted in the uniquely human ability to perceive time and plan for the future. Anxiety is connected to the deep-seated, primal fear centers of our brain. All living beings can feel fear. When we're afraid, we react in a way that keeps us safe. That's good. But the human brain takes this one step further. Instead of being afraid of things happening right now, anxiety is a fear of the future. It's a fear of what's possible. Anxiety catalyzes us to take action in ways that keep us safe and protected from the bad things that *might* happen. The fear of losing the race helps our teen plan their route and remember to warm up their ankles; the fear of not getting accepted to the school they want helps our teen create a college-essay writing plan and stick with it; the fear of embarrassing ourselves in front of our former high-school classmates prompts us to get in shape before the reunion—and so forth.

Anxiety also directs hormones to assist us in the actions we take. A teen who is anxious about an upcoming exam may have just enough adrenaline to help them stay awake and sharpen their focus while studying. When we're anxious about a vague and uncertain future, we take action in ways that have the highest likelihood of keeping us safe and protected. We angle for better jobs and living environments. We try to learn as much as possible. We try to make ourselves valuable to our communities, and to form strong social bonds with others. Thus, anxiety is inexorably linked to achievement, success, and preparation for the future.

Also, because we live in an achievement-centered society, pursuing achievement has become the most socially acceptable way to channel our anxiety. The reaction I get from my peers when I say that I stayed up all night writing my book is very different from when I say I stayed up all night watching TV and eating ice cream. Both are outlets for my anxiety, but one gets me praised by my peers and the other elicits concern.

As a highly social species, a lot of human anxiety (and particularly teen anxiety) is related to social acceptance and wanting to prove our worth to our community. Because we live in an achievement-centered culture, we're more likely to be accepted if we're high performers. Teens are particularly susceptible to achievement anxiety because part of their development involves trying to figure out who they are and how they relate to the rest of the world. Even though studies show us that character and emotional intelligence are bigger indicators of success than grades, character and emotional intelligence are hard to measure. Plus, teens catch on quickly to the fact that statements such as "Hi, I'm Dana—I'm a doctor" convey more prestige than "Hi, I'm Dana—I'm a nice person."

There's nothing inherently wrong with wanting to achieve and using achievement as an outlet for anxiety. Where we run into trouble is that almost no one is aware of—or wants to admit—that their drive to succeed is caused by or related to their sense of anxiety and desire to be accepted. This leads to long-term negative outcomes related to anxiety going unnoticed, untreated, or misdiagnosed, as it is in many teens and adults today. When we see poor performance, our reaction, more often than not, is to increase the pressure to succeed rather than to address the underlying emotional issues.

PARENTING: THE PERFECT
OUTLET FOR ANXIETY

The very nature of parenting is centered on preparing our child for the future, a future that is uncertain and impossible to control. There are few instinctual feelings so primal and overpowering as the need to keep our kids safe. Given their vulnerability and extreme dependency, we are driven by a biological need to protect them from harm, both emotionally and physically. It's fertile ground for our anxieties to take root and grow.

Parental anxiety adds a new overlay to our preexisting protective brain system. If our kids are not safe, this causes us extreme emotional distress, so our anxiety systems double down. By protecting our kids, we also protect ourselves from distress. And when we are in a highly protective mode, anxiety is heightened. Parenting literally alters the brain, making it permanently more protective and engendering primal instincts. When we become parents, no matter how experienced or prepared we are, anxiety, in all its protective glory, emerges in some form or another. When our kids are little, we strap them into their car seats to ensure their physical safety, and we child-proof our medicine cabinets and cleaning supplies. In doing this we are not only keeping them safe but also managing our own anxiety, preventing us from "needing to worry." Each time our children progress to a new stage, new protective instincts arise. The dangers facing a newborn are very different from the dangers facing a teenager.

By the time we become parents, our brains have already established ways of managing our anxiety systems (we'll delve into this more later, in part II)—so much so that they've become second nature. The way we manage our anxieties becomes as unnoticeable to us as the anxieties themselves. A lot of us don't even think we have anxiety. That's the thing weak people have; we're just goal-oriented! Like it or not, we all have some form of anxiety, as well as long-practiced ways of managing it. Naturally, these are methods we use as we parent our kids.

TOO MUCH SUGAR

So anxiety is a useful tool that helps us perform at a higher level, achieve things in life, and keep our kids safe. That sounds great; how could it possibly go wrong? Like sugar, anxiety is healthy and helpful in the right doses. When we're tired and need an extra boost, drinking a Coke can be a great way to get that boost. It gives us the energy we need to complete the tasks before us. But if all we're drinking is Coke, then soon we may face problems with our teeth; we may get ulcers, put on weight, or be at higher risk for diabetes. The right amount of sugar—the "sweet spot," if you will—is helpful. Too much of it causes problems. The same goes for anxiety. Levels of anxiety impact performance. Too little, or too much, and our ability to perform drops considerably.

Earlier I gave an example of how anxiety could help a student create and execute a plan for writing their college essay. But what happens to that same student when their anxiety levels are raised to the extent that performance begins to drop? The story of a former patient, Juliet, provides a poignant example.

It's the summer before Juliet's senior year of high school and she is working as a counselor at a local day camp. In the upcoming fall she'll have a schedule jam-packed with academics and extracurriculars. In addition to her full roster of classes, including AP US History ("A-Push"), she intends to audition for the school play, take one last round of SATs, write her Common App essay, and submit her college applications by November 1, for Early Decision.

Juliet planned to devote her nonworking hours that summer to drafting her college essay, studying for SATs, and narrowing down her college preferences. However, from the moment she began her job at the day camp, she spent most of her evenings and weekends meeting up with her new counselor friends, going to the beach, or relaxing in her room. Her college essay drafting plans included taking time to brainstorm essay ideas with her mom, Lee. While they are very much mother and daughter, they enjoy one another's company and have a "friendship" of sorts. They share many interests, particularly a love of trying new foods, recipes, and cooking together. Juliet was looking forward to having her mother's support with the essay, but decided to push their brainstorming sessions off to later in the summer, once her job at the day camp was over.

Juliet wasn't anxious about her college essay. In her mind, she had months and months to prepare; she wanted to enjoy her final high-school summer, learning and bonding with her new friends. Lee did not share Juliet's laissez-faire attitude, and as the summer passed, she became increasingly disappointed and annoyed with her daughter. Juliet was not adhering to her promised plan *at all*.

In reality, Lee was anxious, but she was unaware of her anxiety. Like we all do, Lee directed her anxiety outward—in this case, at her daughter. From Lee's perspective, Juliet was being irresponsible, a procrastinator, and a poor time manager. "If she wants to get into college, she has to put in the work!" Lee would mutter under her breath. She was certain Juliet was underestimating how much time her college essay would take. Additionally, she recalled the previous spring when she'd spent many late nights helping her daughter manage her feelings of being overwhelmed by schoolwork, and calming her down when she was reduced to tears or panicked about completing assignments.

Lee did everything in her power to be supportive and helpful to Juliet. She also felt bad about the excessive demands placed on this generation of kids, and did her best to be patient. But as the weeks passed, Juliet's socializing increased, as did Lee's anxiety. Plagued by the memory of the painful and sleep-deprived nights of the previous spring, Lee was determined not to have a repeat experience. She knew this could be avoided if Juliet completed her work over the summer. Lee wanted Juliet to take the essay as seriously as she did. Translation: Unconsciously, she wanted her daughter to feel as anxious about it as she did.

Conflict began to arise in their relationship when Juliet texted to say that she was going to "hang out with some of the other counselors and wouldn't be home for dinner."

Lee snapped back with "It seems to me that you should be hanging out with your SAT review book, not your friends. And by the way, didn't you ask me to brainstorm essay topics with you tonight?"

"Yeah, sorry. Can you do it tomorrow?" Juliet responded casually.

As Lee had predicted, tomorrow led to tomorrow and tomorrow, and Lee was becoming increasingly frustrated (aka, anxious). The more Lee saw the writing on the wall and anticipated the emotional pain of the fall, the more tactics she tried on Juliet. In turn, Juliet resented her mother's nagging and constant reminders of all that she needed to

do. She started avoiding Lee because she knew that her mother "only
wanted to talk about essays and SATs."

The support and collaboration Juliet was looking forward to regarding her essay had turned into dread. Her mother had successfully passed
on her anxiety about the essay, but not in a way that spurred Juliet to
action. Juliet was anxious about the essay, but she was also anxious
about her mother's reaction to the essay. She felt less comfortable at
home, so she spent more time out with friends, which left less time for
schoolwork once the school year started, which made her more anxious
about her impending workload.

Because of the increased anxiety that came with the addition of pressure from her mom, Juliet's excitement about what she would accomplish during her senior year had turned into a sense of overwhelm.
No longer making plans for how she would accomplish her work, she
avoided dealing with it, letting it pile up. Her anxiety turned into avoidance, which was having a massive impact on her performance.

BUT LEE WAS RIGHT, WASN'T SHE?

Lee's anxious predictions about the future did start to manifest once
Juliet's senior year started. Juliet was, once again, overwhelmed with
work. It's at this point in the story that the savvy parent says, "See! If
only Juliet had listened to her mom in the first place, all of this could
have been avoided." And that is, indeed, the easiest conclusion for parents to come to. "If only our kids did everything we said, then everything would work out fine."

And that, dear reader, is our anxiety talking. Anxiety restricts our
performance in many ways. One of the most notable is that it limits
access to our prefrontal cortex, our "thinking" brain. When we're anxious, our thinking brain assesses the current situation and determines
how to proceed. Its assessment is based completely on past experiences, generalizing them to fit what's happening in the present. In other
words, we become unable to truly see the situation laid out in front of
us. We're only able to see aspects of the situation that reflect our past
experiences. Lee was unable to see her daughter's excitement about
collaborating with her on her college essay; she was only able to see
how her daughter's perceived procrastination would end in disaster. By

taking action to prevent this disaster, Lee not only made Juliet anxious but also quashed the excitement Juliet felt about collaborating with her.

In our sessions together, Juliet spent very little time expressing anxiety over her schoolwork or the college essay itself. Her overwhelm was mostly directed at the increased pressure from her mother. The closeness and "friendship" Juliet had enjoyed with her mother for so long had become tense and strained.

In a word, the overwhelm Lee had feared was created by her measures to prevent it. Had she managed her own anxiety from the beginning, it's likely that Juliet would have welcomed her collaboration with her college essay and, while overworked, wouldn't have succumbed to overwhelm or avoidance with her school work. At least not on the same level. It was Juliet's anxiety about her relationship with her mother that was causing the greatest part of her distress.

This was quickly apparent once Lee joined our sessions that fall. In our work together, Lee grew to recognize and accept her own anxieties over Juliet's school work. She started to act from her values (I want to be there for my daughter) rather than her anxieties (Juliet's going to mess up this college application process). This enabled her to be available to her daughter in a constructive way. She was able to once again help Juliet regulate and contain her anxiety (instead of mirroring and exacerbating it). With her mother available to her as a supporter and collaborator, Juliet's anxiety and overwhelm noticeably decreased. She successfully applied to college, and both she and Lee expressed pride in the content and quality of her application essay.

PARENTING ANXIETY: THE
SELF-FULFILLING PROPHECY

Lee and Juliet's story is emblematic of the relationship between parents, their anxiety, and their teens. Even though they often seem aloof and disinterested, teens are highly attuned to what their parents think and feel. When toddlers fall they often look to their parents, unsure of how to respond. When a parent acts concerned—"Oh no! Are you okay?"— the toddler begins to cry. They have learned, by watching their parents' behavior, that falling is harmful.

Likewise, our teens look to us for guidance on what to be anxious about. Juliet, relatively unconcerned and confident in regard to her college essay, became overwhelmed by her mother's anxiety. Lee's anxiety, though unconscious, communicated to Juliet that her essay was something to be increasingly anxious about. While it's easy to blame Juliet for not being focused enough on her responsibilities, it was ultimately Lee's inability to manage her anxiety that catalyzed Juliet's overwhelm. As I mentioned briefly in the previous chapter, multiple studies have shown that a primary indicator of a teen's well-being is how well their parents manage stress. If Lee had given less credence to her anxiety-generated thoughts (worries), perhaps the whole anxiety spiral could have been avoided.

A SIMPLE SOLUTION

Lee and Juliet had the benefit of therapy, and the common language that the sessions provided them, to work through their situation and come out on top. But, unfortunately, not everyone has the time, money, or access to therapy that makes it a practical option.

How, then, can we learn to manage our worries, and our anxiety, effectively? How can we keep ourselves and our kids in that sweet spot of anxiety that makes our life better without overwhelming us or burning us out? Luckily, incredibly, most parenting anxiety spirals can be easily disrupted when two simple things happen:

1. We accept that we have anxiety.
2. We recognize how our anxiety manifests.

Accepting that we have anxiety is simple (though not always easy). You can do it right now! Just take my word for it, you have anxiety. There, done. And having anxiety is okay; it doesn't make us weak, bad, or wrong. Just human.

Recognizing how our anxiety manifests is a little trickier. That's what the rest of this book is dedicated to helping you do—specifically, how to recognize the way we react to our anxieties in the context of parenting teens. While the specifics of these reactions are always personal to us, there are understandable and recognizable patterns that I've documented in my thirty years of specializing in treating parenting anxiety.

The next chapter breaks down how anxiety, fear, and worries work so we can have a shared vocabulary throughout the rest of the book. Then, in part II, we will examine the different Parent Anxiety Reaction Types (PARTs) so you can recognize the way your worries work, and learn practical ways to reframe them so they will work better for you and your teen(s).

To sum up, here are some truths about anxiety (and worry) to bring with you into the next chapter:

- *It's human.* We all have emotions; we all have anxiety; and we all worry. It is not a reflection of poor character—it's a pre-wired and protective process to ensure our survival.
- *It's everywhere.* Anxiety shows up in different ways, some less obvious than others, and is more present in our lives than we think. Worries are expressions of anxiety, and they can help us to identify when and how it presents.
- *There's a sweet spot.* In appropriate doses, we can harness anxiety and use it to help us. And in disproportionate doses, we can become paralyzed and end up working against our goals.
- *It's personal.* Anxiety is highly individual depending upon our genetics, experiences, and modeling (how our parents managed their anxiety).
- *It can be harnessed.* When we're able to identify our anxiety, tolerate it, and harness it effectively, we and our teens will benefit.

Chapter 3

How Worry Works

"Sometimes the things we do to cope can inadvertently keep a problem going."

—*Psychology Tools*[1]

WORRY AND ANXIETY WARP OUR
PERCEPTION OF REALITY

Stephanie was pressuring—actually, insisting—that her son Jared break up with his girlfriend before leaving for college. Stephanie worried that if Jared remained in this romantic relationship it would preclude him from engaging in college the way he "should," socially and academically. She worried that her son would not be able to handle the transition to college and the demands of schoolwork, *and* maintain a serious romantic relationship. This stemmed from her own college experience, which had been overshadowed by a long-term romance. She felt she hadn't gotten the opportunity to learn and really discover herself in college the way her peers had. She not only worried that the same thing would happen to her son, but if it did happen, and she hadn't done anything to prevent it, she worried she would be filled with feelings of guilt and regret.

So she did everything in her power to break up the high-school romance. She made disparaging comments about the girlfriend, highlighted her imperfections, and refused to allow her in their home. She went so far as to contact the girlfriend, attempting to convince her that her and her son would be better off in college without one another. Stephanie's worries drove her to react disproportionately, and inappropriately, to her son. This created an emotional wedge between them.

It's important to note that up until this point, Stephanie had had no problem with her son's relationship. No one had had a problem with it. It was as healthy and stable as a high-school romance could be. The nature of worry and anxiety isn't to react to the present, what's currently happening, but to react to projected fears about what *might* happen in the future.

Stephanie drew from her own experience, anticipated an issue, worried about it, and reacted to her worries as if they were facts. Her concerns about what might happen in the future changed the way she viewed her son's relationship. Instead of seeing it as relatively healthy and stable, she now saw it as a threat to his well-being.

There are many different ways that our worries change the way we see the world. The psychological term for these phenomena is *cognitive distortions*,[2] but in this book, we may also refer to them as thought distortions, unhealthy thought patterns, thought traps, or simply anxious thoughts. They all boil down to the same thing: the ways our anxiety bends our thinking and perceptions of the world around us.

OUR THOUGHTS, FEELINGS, AND BEHAVIORS CONSTANTLY INFLUENCE EACH OTHER

Anxiety is not the only emotion that warps our perception of reality. All of our feelings do in one way or another. We've all heard the axiom "Love is blind," which means, essentially, that when we're in love we don't see the flaws of the person/place/thing we're in love with. The cognitive distortions that come with anxiety are similar, only instead of making us blind to flaws that exist, they make us see flaws, threats, and dangers that don't exist. Or they highlight existing dangers and make them seem much more threatening than they really are.

Modern cognitive theory tells us that our thoughts, feelings, and behavior all influence and feed on each other all the time. Stephanie's anxiety about her son going to college manifested in concrete worries about how his relationship would impact his experience. Those worries made her more anxious, which in turn made her worry more. All of this manifested in her behavior, driving her to try and separate her son from his girlfriend. She started to say things like "I don't like her," or "She will make you feel guilty about meeting new people." The more she worried, the more she increased her efforts to break them up, going so far as to say "If you stay with her, we won't pay for you to go to college," or "She is not allowed in our home, and we will block her number from your phone."

Unsurprisingly, the more Stephanie tried to break up the couple, the closer and more bonded they became. Having a shared enemy to connect over only deepened their relationship. And the more isolated Jared felt from his mother, the more he leaned on his girlfriend. Stephanie's worries were causing a paradoxical outcome, which made her even more anxious! Stephanie was caught in a classic anxiety spiral. Her anxiety and worries prompted her to try and solve a problem that didn't exist, which wound up creating a problem that made her all the more anxious and worried.

BREAKING THE CYCLE

Because our thoughts, feelings, and behaviors all influence each other, these types of anxiety spirals can be diffused by interrupting any of these three factors:

1. *Feelings*: If Stephanie had realized she had anxiety about her son's relationship and managed those feelings of anxiety, she probably wouldn't have tried to interfere in the relationship.
2. *Behaviors*: If she was anxious but didn't act on her anxieties, instead allowing the relationship to take its natural course, her anxieties about it wouldn't have caused a rift between her and her son.
3. *Thoughts*: If she'd recognized that her worries about what would happen to her son weren't based in the current reality, she could have maintained her view that the relationship was healthy, and that there was, in fact, nothing to be worried about.

The trick to breaking these anxiety spirals is to recognize that they're happening. If we're unaware of them we're essentially powerless to stop them. But before you go on an anxiety spiral hunt, remember that not all anxieties and worries are harmful. If we're constantly paranoid that our anxieties are going to destroy our lives and cause harm to our children, that's just our anxieties being anxious about anxiety. Which is not helpful.

We can't be constantly on the alert, looking out for where our anxieties and worries are causing us to act irrationally. That's okay, because there are usually clear signs that an anxiety spiral is occurring, or is about to occur. Once we learn to recognize those signs, then we can use tried and trusted techniques to disrupt the spiral, hopefully before it gets out of hand.

RECOGNIZING THE SIGNS

Where there's smoke, there's fire. Thank goodness, because if fire didn't release smoke, it would be a lot more dangerous than it is. In a house fire, by the time we come face-to-face with the actual fire, it's probably already spread out of control. Our saving grace is that the smoke is present and often noticeable long before a fire gets out of hand. That's why smoke detectors are so amazing. They're able to detect the warning signs of fire, aka, smoke, and let us know so we can deal with the fire and/or get to safety before it's too late.

Because of anxiety's insidious nature—it's everywhere—it can be hard to notice when we're anxious. Like fire, by the time we notice that we're feeling anxious, it's probably already caused some distress. We need an early detection system, like a smoke alarm, so we can recognize our anxiety when it flares up and deal with it before it's too late.

Well, where there are worries, there's anxiety.

Research indicates that on some level, our thinking brain is always on. If you don't believe me, take a moment now to try and stop thinking. See? You can't. And while we may not always be aware of the deeper layers of feeling influencing our thoughts, we are always—at least vaguely—aware of what we're thinking. Anytime there's a parenting dilemma, anxiety is inevitably present, and anytime anxiety is present, there will be thought distortions present in the form of worries.

Our worries serve as practical access points, enabling us to recognize and manage our anxieties in a way that will allow us to keep them in a healthy range. Detecting our worries, and how they're influencing our behavior, can give us the advance notice we need to effectively deal with our anxiety before it gets out of hand and starts causing problems. Like a smoke alarm, when we notice the warning signs, that doesn't mean that an anxiety spiral is occurring; sometimes we've just burned toast, and all will be okay.

But the following are signs to us that we should dig a little deeper and see if an anxiety spiral is happening so we can disrupt it before it causes too much damage:

When we're internally conflicted

If we're conflicted about what we should be doing, thinking, or feeling, that's a good sign that some sort of anxious thought pattern is occurring. Internal conflict is usually an indicator that we're going or acting against our values.

We all live our lives according to some internalized value system. Even if we're not consciously aware of what our values system is, we all believe there are some right and wrong ways to behave. When it comes to our kids, our values might include something like "I will always show respect for my kids' individuality," "I will always stand up to bullies," or "My child should always have the freedom to speak their mind."

Identifying what our values are is a great way to redirect our behavior when we realize we're having anxious thoughts. If we're not sure how to behave, then behaving according to our values is my recommended place to start. (See appendix for a worksheet to help you identify your values.)

Cognitive distortions often push and pull us to act in ways that go against our internal values system, which then brings up internal conflict. When we notice this is happening, that's a sign to us that an anxiety spiral is occurring, or imminent.

For example, a father I know had concerns about his daughter's friends. He was worried that some of their hangout sessions were actually parties, and that his daughter wasn't being honest about them. He started to surreptitiously check his daughter's jacket pockets, looking for incriminating evidence. That was ultimately what convinced him to sign up for therapy. As he related to me during one of our initial sessions, he caught himself going through his daughter's pockets and thought to himself, "What am I doing?" He was horrified by his own behavior, and that was the wake-up call he needed to change the way he was going about this situation with his daughter.

Unlike external conflicts, internal conflicts can be more difficult to identify within ourselves. Here are some signs that we're feeling internally conflicted:

- Incongruity between values and actions
- Indecisiveness
- Feelings of guilt, or wondering "What am I doing?"
- Feelings of resentment/depletion of emotional resources: "I'm giving more than I'm receiving," or "I resent needing to spend so much time/energy on this issue."
- Experiencing the symptoms of anxiety, such as increased breathing and heart rate, difficulty sleeping and eating
- Nervous fidgeting or twitching
- Trouble concentrating
- Difficulty sleeping
- Obsessive thinking (recurring negative feelings/self-judgments/self-criticism)

When we're outwardly conflicted

If we are getting into frequent arguments, altercations, or causing drama with the people around us, that's also a strong indicator that an anxiety spiral might be occurring. Such was the case with Stephanie. She eventually realized that her behavior wasn't driving her son and his girlfriend apart—it was driving her and her son apart. She was experiencing daily conflicts with her son, resulting in frequent arguments and him pulling away from her. That was her wake-up call that something needed to change.

As Tolstoy famously said, "Happy families are all alike, but every unhappy family is unhappy in its own way."[3] Outward conflict within families is unique and manifests in a variety of ways. It can be hard to pin down what "conflict" looks like. It's not as simple as saying "We have frequent arguments." For some families—I have a New York Italian family in mind—arguing is a part of their day-to-day functioning and doesn't have an unhealthy influence on their dynamic. In my family, we tend toward passive aggression, so an actual outward argument is usually a clear sign that there's a conflict that needs to be addressed.

Returning to values is a great way to establish if there's a conflict occurring that needs to be addressed. For Stephanie, one of her values was that she wanted her son to always feel like he could talk to her. In her situation, it was clear that the conflict between them was causing her son to feel less and less like he could rely on her. Thus, this was a situation that needed to be addressed and adjusted.

ADDRESSING AND ADJUSTING COGNITIVE DISTORTIONS

To reiterate, the term *cognitive distortions* refers to our mind's tendency to distort reality or view situations and people through an emotionally informed and therefore irrational lens. These irrational thought tendencies are a normal psychological process, and all people experience them to a greater or lesser degree. The more anxious we are and the higher the stakes, the more likely we are to default to these irrational thought tendencies.

When we identify the inward or outward signs that an anxiety spiral is beginning, or already occurring, we can dig into our worries and see if there are cognitive distortions that are perpetuating or worsening our worries/anxiety. And when we recognize our cognitive distortions, there are ways to challenge them and redirect our thinking in more accurate and helpful directions. Identifying cognitive distortions can prevent us from emotionally spiraling, or help us to disrupt a spiral that's already occurring, allowing us to align our actions toward our true goals (and values).

Below is a list of common cognitive distortions that occur when parenting teens and the tools we can use to disrupt them:

1. **Black-and-White Thinking** (also known as all-or-nothing thinking, binary thinking, dichotomous thinking, and polarized thinking): The tendency to think in terms of polar opposites—that is, in terms of the best and worst—without accepting the possibilities that lie between

these two extremes.[4] (Note: All definitions are taken from the American Psychological Association (APA) dictionary.)

We often resort to binary thinking because it feels safe, certain, definitive, and clear-cut. It allows us to view the world in concrete, unambiguous, and finite terms: A person is good or bad, we succeed or we fail, our decisions are right or wrong. Since our conscious brain seeks clarity, certainty, and predictability, we are prone to perceiving things in this way, especially when afraid or anxious. And let's face it—as we've established throughout this book, nuance, ambiguity, and uncertainty can make us feel less stable and more anxious. Thus, we are inclined to reduce complicated, multidimensional, and complex situations into black-and-white terms in order to reduce our anxiety.

Stephanie's* black-and-white thoughts:

- Long-distance relationships are not healthy for college students.
- College students who have long-distance romantic relationships are unable to fully engage in college life.

* While there is overlap between cognitive distortions, it's unlikely that one person is affected by many different cognitive distortions at once. Usually, individuals favor one or two in a given situation. For simplicity's sake, I'll be using Stephanie's situation for all of the examples, exploring what these cognitive distortions would hypothetically look like if she engaged in them.

How to challenge black-and-white thinking: Fact-checking[5]

When we are anxious, we are prone to conflating our opinions with facts about the world. We believe that our thoughts are "truths." If we believe our cognitive distortions are facts, this can cause us to act irrationally. By asking ourselves, "Is this statement a fact or an opinion?" We can start to differentiate fact from opinion and examine the validity of our beliefs, shifting our understanding from objective to subjective (This is a *fact* vs. This is a *perspective*).

If Stephanie had fact-checked the statement "Long-distance relationships are not healthy for college students," she might have found examples of the many college students who have healthy long-distance relationships; or she might have learned that having a long-distance relationship can catalyze personal growth in college students, whether or not the relationship survives long-term.

2. **Catastrophizing** (seeing the worst-case scenario): To exaggerate the negative consequences of events or decisions.[6]

People are said to be catastrophizing when they think that the worst possible outcome will occur from a particular action, in a particular situation, or when they feel as if they are in the midst of a catastrophe in situations that may be serious and upsetting but are not necessarily disastrous. The tendency to catastrophize can unnecessarily increase levels of anxiety and lead to maladaptive behavior.

Stephanie's catastrophizing thoughts:

- Because they spend time together now means she'll be too clingy and will take up all of his time in college, and he won't be able to focus on his studies or make new friends.
- Having a long-distance girlfriend will ruin his college experience.

How to challenge catastrophizing: Decatastrophizing[7]

This technique is a way of challenging catastrophic thinking by using a series of questions. Since catastrophic thoughts are an overestimation of the likelihood of an event and an underestimation of our ability to cope with a situation that might happen, we can "decatastrophize" by asking ourselves questions like:

- What is the worst thing that could happen?
- How likely is it that this worst-case scenario will happen?
- How would I deal with it if it were to happen?

These techniques are helpful because they encourage us to look at our thoughts from a less extreme perspective. We can evaluate the proportional likelihood that a situation might happen and consider the range of coping skills we might use to manage it. For example, statements like, "I will never pass this test, and I'll never forgive myself if I do fail" make us more anxious, which impedes our ability to concentrate, thus diminishing our confidence. One might say, "The likelihood that I'll fail the test is pretty slim. I may not do as well as I'd hoped, but I've never actually failed a test before, so I probably won't fail this one now."

Had Stephanie used decatastrophizing techniques, she would have remembered that her son was not a passive participant in his relationship. He has a strong sense of self and a commitment to participating in college academics and activities. If his girlfriend were to become too demanding and clingy and start to "ruin" his college experience, it is likely that he would stop being satisfied with the relationship and would address that with her directly.

All rainstorms are not hurricanes and all headaches are not brain tumors. These are catastrophic thoughts.

3. **Overgeneralizing** (also occurs in stereotyping): A cognitive distortion in which an individual views a single event as an invariable rule, so that, for example, failure at accomplishing one task will predict an endless pattern of defeat in all tasks. Such thoughts commonly include broad sweeping statements using words like "always" or "never."[8]

Stephanie's overgeneralizing thoughts:

- In the run-up to prom and high-school graduation, Jared's girlfriend started texting him more often. Stephanie's overgeneralization caused her to believe that these recent communications were emblematic of the girlfriend's typical behavior—that she was "always" texting him, "never" left him alone—and that when they went to college, she would expect to be in "constant" communication. Such feelings prompted Stephanie to try and put an end to the relationship before it escalated to a worse state.

How to challenge overgeneralizing: Word replacement[9]

Word replacement is a useful way to challenge a variety of thought distortions. It first requires that we recognize when we are using extreme, absolute, literal terms that do not accurately reflect the facts of the situation. Words like *always* and *never* are common red flags. They are limiting and leave no room for reconsideration, flexibility, or specification.

Words matter, and they can strongly affect our understanding, perception, and feelings about a person or situation. The mere substitution of words can shift one's perceptions, feelings, and actions. Replacing words like *always* and *never* with *rarely, sometimes, frequently,* or *often* makes our thinking more accurate and allows for more flexibility and room for change in our thoughts, feelings, or behaviors.

In the heat of the moment, an angry parent may scold, "You *never* study for tests!" Such a statement is inaccurate, blaming, and shaming (shame is often the by-product of such statements). If a parent replaced these words with "I'm used to seeing you at your desk doing your schoolwork. These past two months, you have rarely been at your desk. What's up?" it would lead to a much more productive interaction with their child.

When Stephanie would say "You're always on the phone with her," Jared's natural response would be "No, I'm not." If Stephanie had changed her language to "She's called the past three nights when you were eating dinner," Jared could have responded, "I will ask her not to call at dinnertime." By presenting a more accurate picture, Stephanie could have created more room for problem-solving and flexible thinking with Jared.

4. **Magnification and Minimization**: These terms refer to errors in evaluation that are so extreme they constitute cognitive distortions. They are usually present in our tendency to exaggerate imperfections and mistakes and minimize achievements and strengths.[10]

This mind-set can lead to chronic feelings of inadequacy and dissatisfaction. When parents or teens focus exclusively on or choose to magnify a negative detail, it infects their view, like putting on a pair of colored glasses and believing that everything they see is actually that color.

Stephanie's magnifying and minimizing thoughts:

- Stephanie magnified the negative aspects of her son's relationship (the threat to his college prospects and experience, how much time his girlfriend "demanded" of him) and minimized the positive aspects (their mutual love and respect, the increased security, comfort, and self-esteem Jared demonstrated since they had started dating, and the obvious joy he felt when around her).

How to challenge magnification and minimization: Socratic questioning

Socratic questioning uses a series of focused, open-ended questions that encourage reflection, self-awareness, and understanding of the sources of our thoughts and perspectives.[11]

Therapists might refer to this as "making the unconscious conscious." These questions help us to gain greater clarity on the origins of our beliefs, behavior, and feelings. When we understand *why* we think, feel, and act in the ways we do, we can better communicate with ourselves and others. It empowers us to manage our emotional responses and ultimately be in control of ourselves rather than allowing our anxieties to control us.

Such questions include, but are not limited to:

- What do I mean when I say _____?
- What other ways might I look at this?
- How might someone else interpret/respond to this situation?

By asking these questions of herself, Stephanie could have expanded her thinking and become more open-minded about the relationship. By considering other perspectives, it's likely she would have recognized how limited (and inaccurate) her working interpretation of the relationship was. She may have even considered that having the relationship could ease her son's transition into college, or that having a relationship that enhances his self-esteem could help him succeed at school.

5. **Jumping to Conclusions**: This is characterized by believing that something will happen based on a gut feeling. Individuals with this unrealistic thought pattern also strongly believe that certain people will behave in a certain way, as if they can read minds or predict the future.[12]

Stephanie's conclusions:

- Jared's girlfriend is toxic, and her toxic behavior will ruin his college experience.
- She will demand that he visit her often and insist that he remain in contact with her in lieu of engaging in class, extracurriculars, or new friendships.

How to challenge jumping to conclusions: Identifying triggers

Identifying triggers is a method of knowing ourselves, our histories, and our emotional vulnerabilities. It connects our past vulnerabilities and sensitivities (often related to traumatic past emotional experiences) to our current experiences. Identifying triggers takes time, self-reflection, and introspection. We should take this time when we find ourselves having an emotional response that seems particularly disproportionate to the situation. For example, when Stephanie felt panic and fear, this was a disproportionate emotional response to the situation of her son having a relationship and planning for college.

When we notice a disproportionate emotional response, we can:

- Reflect on the feeling: What was our physiological response (the physical sensations)?
- Retrace the experience: When did we begin having the feeling?
- Recall what happened just before we noticed the feeling: What were we thinking? Was there an immediate event or comment that set us off?
- Identify an instance from the past in which we had a similar emotion or physiological feeling: Is there anything familiar about the feeling?
- Try to identify themes or patterns between instances: Can we draw connections between past and current responses?

This is a difficult and complicated process to figure out on one's own, and often requires the help of a trusted individual or mental health professional. It can be helpful to write down experiences in a journal and/or discuss our experiences with an objective person.

Stephanie had an obvious trigger. She herself had had a bad experience with her long-distance college relationship. Because Jared's situation was similar to her own, it triggered memories and correspond-ing negative feelings from her own experience, and she responded to Jared's situation as if it were her own. She was unable to differentiate the past from the present.

Once Stephanie recognized this, she was able to view the situation much more objectively and was able to identify many differences between her situation in college and her son's. He was much healthier emotionally, as was his relationship. He and his girlfriend had estab-lished a habit of open and honest communication with one another, and had agreed that they would reevaluate their relationship once they got to college. After identifying her trigger, Stephanie was able to notice when she became triggered and remind herself that her son was healthy and capable of making good decisions.

6. **Belief Bias** (deep-seated beliefs or "should" statements): The tendency to accept our conclusions as true because they are believable (or because we *want* to believe them) rather than because they are logi-cally valid.[13]

These conclusions are heavily influenced by our core beliefs, which can be thought of as our implicit answers to the question, "What has life taught you about yourself, other people, or the world?" We often hold core beliefs as truths about ourselves, the world, or other people, but it's important to remember that they are opinions, not facts.

Stephanie's belief bias:

- College freshmen should not maintain romantic relationships with high-school partners.
- Before attending college, partners should break up.
- Long-distance relationships are unhealthy.

How to challenge belief bias: Socratic questioning[14]

As with magnification and minimization, discussed earlier in this chap-ter, Socratic questioning helps us to gain greater clarity on the origins of our beliefs, behavior, and feelings.

Questions that are helpful to start with when seeking to challenge belief bias are:

- Might other people have different interpretations of this situation?
- Where did my beliefs come from?
- Are these beliefs accurate/applicable to the current situation?

If she had asked these questions, Stephanie would have been able to see her beliefs as opinions or unique perspectives rather than universal truths. If Stephanie had recognized her beliefs as opinions, rather than facts, she would have been free to act differently toward her son's relationship. If it's a fact that long-distance relationships are unhealthy, then it would only be logical for her to try and keep her son out of one. But in realizing that it's not a fact, it's no longer necessary for her son and his girlfriend to break up in order for her son to have a healthy life.

7. **Labeling** (lingering judgments): The attachment of labels to ourselves or others in response to a behavior or event. These labels are usually negative or destructive and are reflective of character.[15] This labeling shuts down communication and leaves minimal opening for improvement or exploration (e.g., "He's a brat." "I'm a bad parent." "She's lazy.").

STEPHANIE'S LABELS:

- Jared's girlfriend is clingy and demanding.

How to challenge labeling: Nonjudgmental stance

Labels are judgments we distill down and apply to things so we can remember them later.[16] We judge that someone is being lazy, so we label them lazy. A preoccupied coworker doesn't greet us in the morning, so we label them rude.

There are many instances when judgments (immediate assessments) are helpful and necessary, but judgments can also elicit strong emotions. Lingering judgments, like labels, can shape and distort our thinking long after the moment when they might have been useful has passed.

By default we live our lives in a judgmental stance, often assigning opinion, preference, approval, value, or criticism to what's going on.

A nonjudgmental stance is an intentional mind-set that says "I'm paying attention to the present moment and the present situation and leaving my past judgments out of it." A nonjudgmental stance is observational, aware, neutral, and focused on the facts of a situation. When in a nonjudgmental stance, we purposefully do not include descriptors that could impact interpretation, like good, bad, lazy, smart, stupid, or clingy.

Judgmental: She is wearing an ugly/pretty/expensive/etc., dress.

Nonjudgmental: She is wearing a dress.

Judgmental: I have so many difficult tasks to do today.

Nonjudgmental: I have to complete the following three tasks today.

A nonjudgmental stance is helpful because it removes the emotional charge that stems from our interpretations, and by doing so, prevents the cascade of an anxiety spiral. When Jared was texting with his girlfriend and Stephanie would think, "Jared's texting with his girlfriend—she's so clingy and demanding," there would naturally be a negative emotion cast over her experience of watching her son text with his girlfriend. However, if Stephanie were to see Jared texting with his girlfriend and think, simply, "Jared's texting with his girlfriend," there would be no negative emotion accompanying the experience. This would leave her open to being proactive, rather than reactive, when approaching her son.

SOLUTIONS FOR COGNITIVE DISTORTIONS

1. Fact-checking (see page 38)
2. Decatastrophizing (see page 39)
3. Word replacement (see page 40)
4. Socratic questioning (see page 44)
5. Identifying triggers (see page 43)
6. Nonjudgmental stance (see page 45)[17]

As you may have noticed, there is a great deal of overlap between the cognitive distortions listed and their solutions. All cognitive distortions essentially boil down to the same thing: the ways our emotions distort our perception of reality. The various names and distinctions we give them are simply useful ways to think about our thought patterns. Labeling them may help you to identify them when they occur. (See, labeling can be useful!)

The distortions and solutions listed in this chapter are the ones I've found to be the most helpful when treating my patients, although there are many other names for cognitive distortions and multiple ways of challenging them. There is a list of resources in the back of this book if you'd like to read further on the subject. It's important to realize, however, that for all practical intents and purposes, there is no need to be quite so clinical in identifying your specific thought traps. The key thing is to pay attention to, and become more aware of, your thoughts. When you notice that your interpretations are causing you trouble, or that they are not quite lining up with reality, then it's time to apply some of these tools and see if you can identify where your worries are leading you astray.

PART II

The PARTs Parents Play

As part of our ongoing quest to effectively parent, we try to ensure that we are responsive to our teens and that our parenting aligns with our values rather than merely reacts to our anxieties.

In chapter 2, we took a deep dive into anxiety, and in chapter 3, we identified and explored its many cognitive iterations—the ways that our worries impact our thoughts and perspectives.

Another way that we can interrupt an anxiety spiral is by examining our behaviors—the actions we take in our day-to-day parenting. Part II of this book provides examples of the roles that parents play in their teens' achievements, or, more specifically, the role our anxiety plays in our teens' achievements. Based on cases in my practice, this section profiles thematic ways that parental anxiety manifests in teens' achievements—what I call Parent Anxiety Reaction Types (PARTs). These eight archetypes illustrate the role that parents' achievement anxieties can play, often unwittingly derailing interactions with their teens.

Each case illustrates how parents' self-reflection, identification, and management of their anxiety helped them to guide their children in accordance with their values. Essentially, parents learned how to respond to their teen rather than react to their worries. This empowered them to guide their teens and themselves in a values-aligned, self-aware, intentional, and, most importantly, effective way.

HARNESS YOUR ANXIETY TO DIRECT
YOUR PARENTING DECISIONS

Each PART example includes a description of the anxiety reaction type; its perks (qualities you can draw on when making achievement-related decisions) and pitfalls (qualities you should avoid when making achievement-related decisions); anxiety triggers; common cognitive distortions; and ways that awareness and acceptance can help to harness your anxiety to benefit your teens and yourselves.

The purpose of this discussion is to help you identify with some of the hidden ways that anxiety can rear its head even in your most well-intentioned parenting efforts, and how once you recognize your anxiety and shift your thinking, you will be able to shift your parenting decisions to align with your values, rather than merely reacting to your anxieties. This will improve your relationship with your teens and your teens' overall well-being.

As you read, you will likely identify with aspects of each PART. Each anxiety reaction type is not written in stone; consider them as frameworks for understanding, not concrete and rigid definitions. They offer some common styles of managing anxiety, and some reference points for the ways that anxiety might be inadvertently driving your decisions. Note the steps that the parents in each case study took to understand their anxiety process and the ways they harnessed their anxiety to achieve their actual goals, and to help their children achieve authentically. Anxiety awareness helped these parents make small changes that had a large impact on their teens' trajectory and overall mental health.

Each of the following chapters explores one of these eight PARTs:

1. **Sculptors** see their teen's lack of skills as severely detrimental to their future. Through academics, extracurricular activities, and even therapy, they work to shape their teen into a perfectly well-rounded product.
2. **Game Show Contestants** are certain that each parenting decision has a definitive right and wrong answer. Their thinking can become very binary (e.g., "If I don't hire a tutor, she'll fail"). They may become paralyzed with the fear of making a wrong decision. And even after they've made a decision, they can become obsessed with wondering if they've made the wrong one (e.g.,

"We chose school x, but maybe he would have done better at school y").

3. **Crowd-Pleasers** are tuned in to the cultural norms. They are both competitive and conforming. They look to their teen's peers to determine what milestones their teen should be achieving at this time, while also viewing them as the ones their teen will have to "beat" at school and in the job market. They make decisions that align with what others are doing (e.g., urging their teen to take Mandarin even though they enjoy Spanish) in order to be competitive and not fall behind. Their motto is, "If they're doing it, we need to, too."

4. **Avoiders**, unlike other PARTs, may appear more relaxed and laid-back. Their motto is "Everything will work out." They focus on their teen's day-to-day needs rather than on the long-term implications of decisions. Letting "fate" decide and tending to procrastinate helps to manage their anxiety. If things go wrong, they won't feel responsible because it wasn't a result of their actions; it just "happened."

5. **Clairvoyants** identify their child's gifts and talents (real or imagined) and believe that they will lead them to future success. They make decisions that put their teen on an accelerated course to master their talents.

6. **Shepherds** lead their teens through the linear pastures of childhood, clearing the path to show them the route to success.

7. **Correctors** are self-reflective parents who examine their own childhoods to inform their parenting approach. When faced with an achievement-related decision, they look to the past and the way their parents raised them. Correctors disagree with the choices their parents made and try to prevent their children from going through a similar experience. They are adamant about doing things differently.

8. **Replicators** benefited from their parents' choices. Their motto is, "If it worked for me, it will work for you." They're staunchly dedicated to preserving their family's legacy by doing things the way they've always been done.

Chapter 4

Randy the Sculptor

Randy was at her wits' end with her twenty-year-old daughter, Ellen. On the heels of another "wasted summer," Randy was unable to motivate Ellen to do "anything."

As Ellen entered her junior year at a local college, she claimed to have "absolutely no idea" about her life's direction. She had never worked a part-time job, she was unaware of any areas of interest, and was unable to identify any experiences upon which to draw. According to her mother, Ellen was passive and seemingly unfazed by her stagnation. Randy, on the other hand, was acutely aware of her own growing sense of urgency and was afraid she'd "failed" as a mother. Unfortunately, the topic of what Ellen was going to do after college had become so charged at home that its mere mention caused Ellen to "become hysterical and melt down."

Randy relayed all of this to me during our initial meeting.

"She has nothing, and I mean *nothing*, to put on a résumé—not an internship, a summer job, any experiences, interests, hobbies—nothing! Not only that, she couldn't interview if her life depended on it! She won't even speak to a cashier at a store . . . or any stranger, come to think of it. How is she going to get a job?"

Randy suspected that Ellen's need for therapy was long overdue. During a previous period of heightened stress, while applying to college, Ellen's pediatrician had prescribed an antidepressant that helped her "get through" the process. Yet, up until this point, Randy had believed she could deal with her daughter's challenges on her own.

Since she had always managed Ellen in the past, Randy was now at a loss. Nothing she tried seemed to bring any results.

Randy's situation is emblematic of the struggle many Sculptor parents find themselves in. Accustomed to being able to solve problems on their own, Sculptors often find themselves at a loss when faced with an adolescent they can't seem to shape.

WHO ARE SCULPTOR PARENTS?

The great sculptor Michelangelo famously called himself a liberator of sculptures. He believed that inside every block of marble is a sculpture; all the artist needs to do is remove the extraneous elements.

Sculptor parents have taken this lesson to heart. Inside the block of pure potential that is their child is a great "something" waiting to be released. Unlike Clairvoyants, Sculptor parents don't cling to an unchangeable vision of who their child is supposed to be. They're flexible, and willing to work with whatever they're given.

Sculptors are parent-artists: They believe they can make something from anything—they just need some material to start with. They are typically parents who identify as being self-made. They've successfully sculpted their own lives and trust that those skills will translate over to parenting.

Sculptors are self-directed, detail-oriented, creative problem-solvers that can make things happen. Prone to perfectionism, their acutely discriminating eye can readily identify perceived potential problems.

They keep their anxiety at bay by identifying areas for improvement, or detecting potential problems *before* they can worsen or spiral out of control. They assume a rational, solution-oriented approach and are adept at coming up with ideas, making things work, and following through.

Through their talents, they masterfully round out the edges of their kids' personas and fill in the gaps of résumés, skills, and personalities to prevent these perceived deficiencies from worsening or precluding their teen from enjoying future opportunities. Thus, they build on the existing material presented to them by their kids. Or at least, that's the idea.

Sculptor Perks:

- Detail-oriented: Sculptors have an acutely discriminating eye which enables them to identify areas for improvement.
- Solution-focused: When they perceive a problem, Sculptors use their acquired experience and reasoning to solve the problem.
- Self-assured: From their perfected artistry experience, Sculptors are confident and driven to accomplish their tasks and projects.

MEETING ELLEN

Randy predicted that there was no way Ellen would come to see me without her being there, as well, so we arranged for Randy to accompany Ellen to the initial consultation.

As I greeted this incongruous mother-daughter duo in my waiting room, Randy's eagerness and Ellen's hesitancy were apparent. In anticipation, and practically in unison to my opening the office door, Randy jumped up from the large single seat club chair that she and her daughter were sharing. Dressed in stylish work attire, the petite mother enthusiastically extended her hand, and with a strong New York accent she introduced herself and her daughter to me.

Following her mother's lead, Ellen slowly rose from the chair and positioned her taller body behind her mother, as if wishing to hide.

As they entered the office, Randy sat at the edge of the couch to ensure that her feet were touching the ground, while Ellen sat back and wedged herself between her mother and the couch cushions, as if to camouflage herself between the supports. Dressed in a plain gray oversize sweatshirt, black leggings, and Stan Smith sneakers—a shapeless, nondescript style—Ellen effectively concealed any signs of physical maturation. Her long, straight, medium brown hair provided a curtain-like veil through which she could hide, periodically peeking through to communicate. As her mother reiterated the concerns she had mentioned on the phone, Ellen resisted eye contact, smiled nervously, and giggled softly.

Acutely attuned to her discomfort, I gently asked Ellen to weigh in on her mother's narrative or to offer her own perspective, but she sheepishly defaulted to her mother. Despite Randy's encouragement— "You can answer," or "You don't need me to answer that"—Ellen shrugged and shamefully responded "I don't know," as if a blank slate, unsure how to answer, afraid of getting it wrong, and not knowing where to start.

Randy encouraged, prompted, and cued her daughter to respond, yet whenever Ellen paused, Randy filled in the blanks.

"Believe me, she's not *this* quiet at home. Right, Ellen?"

Peeking through her long strands of hair, Ellen nodded and laughed nervously.

With the confidence and savviness likely cultivated in her long-standing career as a prosecutor, Randy described her many efforts to understand and accept Ellen's passivity while trying, unsuccessfully, to get Ellen to try *anything*.

"She tells me that she wants to get a job one day and figure out what she'd like to do, but she refuses to take any steps toward doing so," Randy said, half-jokingly. "And unfortunately, we don't know of any careers which require you to lie in bed all day and watch Netflix!" Eyebrows raised, she turned to her daughter knowingly. "I think that's what you'd really prefer!"

Looking like she wanted the ground to swallow her up at that moment, Ellen laughed nervously again.

"Believe me," Randy said, glancing at me slightly self-consciously, "I'm not one of those out-of-control New York City parents who pressures her kids and sets ridiculous expectations." Then, turning toward Ellen, "It's not like I'm saying you need to become a neurosurgeon or lawyer—I just want you to show interest in something other than *Gossip Girl*, *Riverdale*, and your bed!"

"I know," Ellen responded sheepishly.

During the following long, pregnant pause, Randy offered more context.

"I've begged her to just *try* the career center. I've offered to introduce her to people that I know in all different fields. I've given her email addresses of people who've offered to talk to her. I even said I'd go with her to talk to these people, but she won't do it. She won't even *try!*"

Here we see the genesis of Sculptor anxiety. They're willing to work with whatever their kids give them, but when they're put in a situation where they feel as if they have no material to work with, they don't know what to do. In the face of Ellen's apparent apathy Randy was lost and confused.

Softening a bit, she said, "Don't get me wrong. In many ways, Ellen is *much* easier to deal with than her younger sister, who can be moody and even mean at times. Ellen is so kind, loving, and easy to be with. We have so much fun hanging out together, just the two of us."

THE SCULPTOR PARENT'S DILEMMA

Randy's dilemma was that Ellen is not a block of marble ready to be shaped by a skillful hand. No child is. They are living, breathing, evolving entities.

Ideally, sculptors chip and polish their material according to its natural contours. Yet, much to her dismay, Randy's material was unresponsive to her finessing. Many parents are frustrated by their teens' unresponsiveness, but this is especially debilitating for Sculptors.

As Randy attempted to chip away at Ellen, she was dismayed to find no sculpture inside, waiting to be liberated. The more she applied her tools, the more she was at a loss for what to do next. Over time she began to wonder if maybe her chunk of marble was defective.

While Sculptors are carefully attuned and discerning parents, when Sculptor tendencies are employed in excess, it can lead to unwitting implications in their children's development. Because her artistic talents had always worked in the past, Randy feared that there was something wrong with her material. Was Ellen simply incapable of taking shape?

Some of Randy's best qualities—confidence, self-assurance, and relentless determination—were exactly what kept her from responding appropriately to Ellen's needs. It never occurred to Randy that it was her method of sculpting that was causing Ellen to be unresponsive. She was so afraid of Ellen's stagnation and anxious that Ellen wouldn't take shape in time that she doubled down on her efforts.

Because Sculptor parents are so self-assured and confident, they often jump to the conclusion that the heart of the problem lies with their kids, rather than their parenting approach. Instead of adjusting what *they* are doing, they just apply more and more pressure or force, believing that if they just do more, work a little harder, their child will eventually respond.

As the child refuses to conform to the Sculptor's expectations, the Sculptor's attempt to shape them may ultimately hamper the child's ability to grow and flourish according to their nature. As was the case with Randy and Ellen.

ELLEN: A HUMAN CHILD, NOT A BLOCK OF MARBLE

Despite my years of experience engaging resistant teens, I found myself scrambling for a way to draw Ellen out. I needed to do some work to meet this painfully self-conscious, timid teen where she was. From what I had been able to glean thus far, she preferred to be hidden, and likely felt alone in her feelings.

So, with little else to build on, I engaged Ellen in a topic that was most familiar and comfortable to her: her admitted area of interest—TV!

"You may not believe this," I said, somewhat hesitant and self-conscious, "but I am embarrassingly out of it when it comes to TV series and movies. I think I have some weird, undiagnosed disorder that prevents me from focusing, staying awake, or following a show."

She looked at me quizzically. "You probably don't have much time to watch TV."

"I appreciate you letting me off the hook, but I *do* have a little time in the evenings. Often I find myself surfing our many channels; there are so many options that it's overwhelming. I don't even know where to start! And in the rare instance that I *do* find something to watch, I can't seem to stick with it, even for one episode. I get distracted, forget what happened, miss half of what they're saying, or fall asleep—even when I'm not tired!"

As I verbalized my feelings, Ellen's posture began to shift. She lifted her head, raised her eyebrows, and smiled, seemingly entertained by my vulnerability and exposed lack of ability with something that came so easily and naturally to her.

"Really?" she said, seeming like she wanted to hear more.

"Don't judge me!" I said, somewhat playfully. "In all seriousness, it's pretty embarrassing. It makes me dread when someone asks what series I'm watching. I feel so out of it, like I live under a rock. I have nothing to contribute when it comes to pop culture! A lot of times when I do start watching a series, I'm so many seasons behind everyone else that I can't offer much. I'd like to get into a show, but every time I've tried, it doesn't work."

As I shared my genuine insecurity about my inability to participate in an activity which seemed so natural and enjoyable to others, and kept me from fitting in or contributing to conversations, Ellen appeared interested and visibly less tense. Perhaps I was articulating her feelings that she was unable to verbalize. So, I continued.

"I actually need someone who is familiar with what's going on to give me the CliffsNotes version for the most popular shows. Perhaps you could help me? Maybe with your introduction, I'd feel a little more primed to dive into a show?"

Ellen swept her hair from her face, exposing large green eyes and a beautiful wide grin with pronounced and endearing dimples. Perhaps these hidden facial features were emblematic of hidden personality features within her.

"What shows do you like to watch?" I asked.

"I like a lot of things, even some of the older stuff. I like certain reality shows, like *Dancing with the Stars* and *Kardashians*. Oh, yeah, and I love mysteries, especially medical mysteries. It depends on what I'm in the mood to watch, but there are shows like *Grey's Anatomy*, I never get tired of watching. I can recite practically every *Friends* episode by heart!"

"Yes!" I said, as if I had won the lottery. I asked if she would consider sharing her expertise with me, and she agreed. While she might not have expected a Netflix-themed initial consultation, Randy seemed to appreciate Ellen's noticeable comfort and willingness to participate in therapy from that point on.

Over the next few months, Netflix became the vehicle through which our relationship developed. This familiar topic offered a predetermined path and direction in which Ellen felt safe to assume the driver's seat. Ellen didn't need to come up with any *new* material; she simply conveyed the preexisting plotlines of her favorite medical mysteries and teen dramas. With her leading and me following, we sifted through content and characters; we sought and connected clues which helped to solve TV mysteries; we analyzed characters' emotions, and hypothesized about the inner workings of their dynamics and relationships.

Through this exploration we periodically, and with increasing frequency, applied her insights about the characters to herself: her lack of confidence, her paralyzing feelings of inadequacy and incompetence, her chronic helplessness, and her unnatural dependency on her mother. Sometimes indirectly we even touched upon the oft-disavowed parts of herself that yearned for motivation, competence, and self-reliance.

Each week, Ellen came to the sessions on her own. Often arriving early with a lilt in her step, she'd enter my office. As she removed her coat, before sitting down, she'd exclaim "OMG! You will not believe what happened! I couldn't wait to tell you . . . " and she'd be off, enthusiastically sharing plotline twists and emerging themes from the latest episodes of the shows we discussed. She knew I was relying on her updates to keep me up to speed, and she reliably filled each session with the material I was unable to ascertain on my own. She had the goods that I was waiting for!

Contrary to the existing surface narrative—that Ellen was lazy and preferred to have things done *for* her—Ellen was connecting to part of herself that found fulfillment in the role of teacher, helper, and expert. She seemed almost giddy as she helped me with my TV deficiency. For the first time, she was experiencing herself differently from the painfully dependent role she had assumed with her mother.

Unlike her usual quiet milquetoast presentation, we were uncovering a feisty, sensitive, and funny adolescent who feared abandonment and yearned for connection and competence. As it turned out, her seeming lack of motivation and paralysis were rooted in her highly perfectionistic expectations, her intolerance for mistakes, and the corresponding humiliation she believed she would experience when she ultimately failed.

Yet, in her role as the Netflix content expert, Ellen began to see another possibility. She recognized and cherished the deep satisfaction and empowerment she felt from her growing self-knowledge, and she expressed motivation and curiosity about her inner workings. For the first time, she was challenging her deep-seated beliefs about herself and considering updating her long-standing narrative. It was empowering!

Ellen was eager to share her insights with her mother—her realizations about her debilitating anxiety and its manifestations in their problematic dynamic. And in doing so, Randy became aware of the ways that Ellen's anxiety catalyzed her own anxiety.

RANDY: A SCULPTOR PARENT

As a single mother and highly accomplished attorney, Randy approached her work and parenting with energy, competence, and capability. Rarely appearing overwhelmed, she seemed to juggle her daily responsibilities with confidence and self-assuredness. In fact, she built a life for herself despite little parental guidance or financial resources in her upbringing. As an adolescent of the 1960s, she was inspired to be ambitious and self-sufficient. She was determined to prove her equality to her older brother, and so, like him, she pursued a legal career.

"When I was her age, I was looking at law schools, studying for the LSAT exam, and negotiating with my parents about financing graduate school. I can't imagine *not* having done that! I couldn't wait to get out from under my parents' roof, to be on my own and make a life for myself!"

She paused, as if trying to connect the many dots, struggling to make sense of this complex mother–daughter relationship.

"I mean, I may have been more outgoing and less shy than Ellen, but she is a smart kid. She could do *anything* in math or science—they come so easily to her—but she has no interest! Which is fine, but she has *no interest in anything!* And believe me, we've tried everything."

"Clearly, you have so much to offer," I validated. "I imagine this has been very frustrating for you."

It was Ellen's perceived noninterest that was the most frequent trigger for Randy's Sculptor anxiety. With a lack of source material, sculptors often find themselves at a loss. "How am I supposed to create a sculpture when there's nothing inside my block of marble waiting to be set free?"

"You know, in New York City you can find *anything* for kids," Randy said. "The options are endless!" She looked at me knowingly. "When she was very little, I was so excited for her to try everything, to see what she enjoyed. And if something didn't stick, I was determined to keep trying!"

She held her hand up and lifted each finger as she enumerated her many efforts over the years.

"I enrolled her in a kids' soccer program, and she stood on the side-lines and refused to play. I figured that team sports were too overwhelming for her, so I enrolled her in figure skating, thinking that something more individualized would appeal to her—but no. She complained about the cold, and the teacher. She could not have been less enthusiastic. So then I figured she might like something less physical and more creative, so I enrolled her in a small neighborhood art class. Surprise. She didn't like that either. Creative writing—no. She hated piano, and she even resented having to play the recorder in school. Nothing!"

Empathizing with how frustrating this would be as a parent, I reflected, "Wow, you have tried so hard to get some activity off the ground. You have such admirable perseverance!"

She desperately tried to find a starting place for her sculpture, but no clear vision presented itself. Throughout middle school, Randy strongly encouraged Ellen to participate in school activities and afterschool clubs. But if she agreed to sign up for one, on the scheduled day she would feign illness, or claim to be too tired, or not in the mood to attend.

"After years of doing this, I couldn't battle about it anymore. While these were meant to be activities for her, she was only doing them for me! That defeated the whole purpose. I wanted her to do something, but I wasn't going to force her." Sounding resigned, she added softly, "When she was younger, it was easier and more acceptable to rational-ize—like, she's shy, or she doesn't like change. But now she's twenty years old!"

I said, "Yes. On the verge of adulthood, the stakes seem much higher."

"I try to build her confidence, since she has none," Randy said. "I tell her that she's smart and likable, but that she needs to *try* to talk to strangers, *try* the career counseling office at school . . . just *try*."

Typically, like a true Sculptor, Randy felt that with hard work and determination, she was going to make things happen. Yet, when it came to Ellen, she was stumped. She had little to work with. She wondered why she couldn't get her smart kid, who had every conceivable advantage, to make something happen.

As we peeled back the layers of Randy's hard-earned frustration, we uncovered her unbearable feelings of powerlessness and ineffectiveness—vulnerabilities so uncomfortable that she typically acted on them before she was even aware they existed.

UNDERSTANDING THE SCULPTOR'S ANXIETY

For the Sculptor, who is used to being able to shape and create the world according to their desires, nothing triggers a sense of anxiety faster than feelings of powerlessness. They're so competent, so used to being able to overcome every challenge with a mix of intelligence, creativity, hard work, and skill, that when they're met by a seemingly insuperable barrier, they're not only frustrated by the challenge presented, but their entire identity is called into question.

This is particularly true for Sculptor parents. They think, If I can't solve this challenge facing my child, then what kind of a parent am I?

Sculptor anxiety is triggered by:

- Inaction—If they're not given anything to do or any materials to work with, Sculptors are left at a loss.
- Unresponsiveness and Passivity—Sculptors need progress; they crave it. Their worst nightmare is to spend years chipping away at a block of marble only to find that it's remained entirely unchanged.
- Ineffectiveness—Sculptors are used to being extremely effective. Faced with the prospect that their methods are failing them, they become desperate.

The Sculptor deals with their anxiety by:

- Doubling down and increasing their efforts
- The more they see a lack of progress, the harder they try and the more pressure they exert. They may do so by hiring professionals or finding new activities to introduce the child to.
- Being critical of their child and pointing out the perceived areas for improvement
- Pointing out what their child is doing "wrong"

- Comparing them to other children that are having more notice-able success
- Trying to "shame them into succeeding"

Because Sculptors have been so successful in their own lives, they're prone to believing that their way is the right way—that there is only one correct way to go about things. While they are open to trying new things, they never question their process.

Sculptors cling to the false notion of "If I keep working at this, I will find a solution." However, it is their process—their method of trying to shape their child—that is ineffective. To keep working at it with the same method is simply exacerbating the problem.

While Randy did try suggesting a bunch of different activities to Ellen, in an effort to spark an interest, the *way* she went about getting Ellen to try those things was the same. What Randy didn't see was that Ellen's process was different from hers. It wasn't that Ellen hadn't tried the right thing; it's that her process wasn't being respected.

Sculptors are used to working with marble, so they just chisel away. When their material doesn't respond, they chisel harder. But when their child isn't a block of marble, chiseling harder doesn't help.

Randy thought that Ellen's unresponsiveness was the problem, when it was actually a sign that her approach was ineffective. Ellen was giv-ing something back; Randy just couldn't see it.

Most of the time, it's the things Sculptors overlook that are actually the sculpting materials they have to work with—the actual opportuni-ties for growth.

Such was the case with Randy and Ellen.

THE ANXIETY SPIRAL

"I think that we can see a pattern here," I suggested. I knew that if Randy could track the trajectory of her anxious feelings, the cor-responding thoughts, and her behaviors, she would be better able to help her daughter. She could respond to Ellen, rather than react to her own anxiety.

As we examined Randy's anxiety, she tracked her corresponding thoughts. As her anxiety rose, she resorted to common thought traps like black-and-white thinking and catastrophizing. Randy slowly tapped into how uncomfortable and terrified she felt by Ellen's inertia.

"What am I supposed to do—let her lie in bed all day? I can't watch her do nothing. It drives me *crazy*! I'd be failing her as a mom if I let her do this!"

In a knowing, fellow-mom tone, I said, "As a parent, this is one of our greatest fears. It is so painful to think about, and we're determined not to let that happen!"

"She could end up being the adult who lives in the NYC equivalent of her mother's basement! If I didn't get her out of bed, she wouldn't get up. It's unbelievable!"

"That is a scary worst-case scenario," I agreed. "You feel like the onus is on you to create a life for her, to motivate her so as to prevent this from happening."

"Well, what am I supposed to do? She is almost a college graduate, and she has no idea what she wants to do. Isn't it my job as her parent to help her find out?"

Understandably, Ellen's passivity and lack of interest was anxiety-producing for Randy. Randy needed some sort of observable progress to latch on to, and the lack of it regularly sent her into a spiral.

In previous sessions, I had reviewed human physiological fear responses and the way our minds try to preempt future recurrences of emotional discomfort—the conditioned behaviors commonly called "fight, flight, or freeze." Randy and I recognized that she and Ellen had differing anxiety responses that played off of one another and created an unhelpful dynamic between them.

Randy's response to anxiety was to fight. Like most Sculptors, she is a fighter through and through. When she feels anxious, Randy reaches for her reliable Sculptor tools and works on her product—aka, Ellen. Ellen, on the other hand, freezes, which catalyzes Randy's anxiety, prompting her to act.

Essentially, Randy fought Ellen's inaction with problem-solving and taking charge. The more anxious she was about her daughter, the more action she took. Likewise, every time Randy approached Ellen with her bag of tools, Ellen's anxiety would spike, prompting her to freeze.

Randy and Ellen's respective anxieties were caught in a cycle, a feedback loop which created the opposite response in Randy to what

Ellen needed. Randy's attempts to help her daughter were inadvertently reinforcing Ellen's helplessness.

In her efforts to construct an experience for Ellen, she was unknowingly conveying the message "You're right. You're unable to do this task. *I* need to do it for you. You are as incapable and incompetent as you feel, even for seemingly easy tasks. I will do it for you," essentially reinforcing "You need me."

As Randy executed tasks for Ellen with ease, she reinforced Ellen's sense of inadequacy. In Randy's efforts to emphasize the task's simplicity, she'd say things like "This is *not* a big deal. It's so simple," reinforcing just how inadequate Ellen was, and how different compared to Randy. What Ellen heard and internalized was "You are unable to do even the simplest of tasks. You are so far behind your peers. If you can't talk to the cashier at the pharmacy, how could you possibly do X, Y, or Z?" Meanwhile, Ellen's constant "I don't knows" reinforced Randy's feelings of powerlessness.

Given how far behind and delayed Ellen seemed to her, Randy felt like she was playing an ongoing game of catch-up. She was aware of Ellen's peers "passing her by" and was desperate for her daughter to gain some ground.

SCULPTING ANXIETY

Our kids *do* learn from us, for better or for worse. Because of their intuitive nature, they often pick up on emotional lessons before intellectual ones. Randy was trying to teach Ellen, "Look, here are all of the things you can do—you just need to do them!" But the lesson Ellen was learning from Randy's teaching attempts was actually "Here are all of the things for you to feel anxious about!"

Because Randy was unconscious of her own anxieties, she was inadvertently teaching Ellen to be anxious about all of the same things she herself was anxious about. Randy was sculpting Ellen—just not in the way she thought.

Common Sculptor pitfalls:

- Inhibiting the child's growth: Randy's well-intended efforts to build or improve upon Ellen thwarted Ellen's ability to develop the essential confidence that comes from doing so
- Impatience: Eager to see progress, Sculptors may accelerate the process, unwittingly bypassing important developmental skills.
- Because Randy believed Ellen was "behind," she doubled down on her efforts to "catch her up." By doubling down, she increased Ellen's fear and continually triggered her impulse to freeze.
- Lowering the child's self-esteem: Nobody likes to be told what to do, that they are not "good enough," or that they need to do things differently. Ellen, like many kids of Sculptor parents, heard Randy's good intentions as criticisms. This, in turn, reinforced Ellen's sense of inadequacy and shame.
- Preventing the child from learning life skills because Sculptors have such a hard time tolerating their own anxiety, they often take the reins from their kids when it comes to performing certain tasks. Since Randy took over every time Ellen didn't "do it right," Ellen never learned how to act independently.

FACING THE ANXIETY

Through our sessions, Ellen developed the ability to articulate and share her inner experience. She was able to see how Randy would provoke her anxiety, causing her to freeze.

Ellen explained this to Randy during one of our family sessions.

"You don't understand. You say that it's not a big deal to talk to a stranger, but the minute the person looks at me, my mind goes blank. I can't think of what to say. I'm like a deer caught in the headlights. I'm so embarrassed, and I know they think I must be weird. This makes me even more self-conscious."

After a brief pause, Ellen continued.

"I know you're trying to help me, and I need your help, but a different kind."

As Randy listened to Ellen's detailed descriptions of her anxiety and its corresponding narratives, Randy felt her own anxiety rise. This, in turn, led her to feel her previously unconscious, overpowering, reactive impulse to jump in and problem-solve. In real time, she realized that while acting on this impulse had helped her to avoid experiencing her own anxiety, it had also interfered with Ellen's development. By problem-solving for Ellen and doing everything for her, Randy was essentially preventing Ellen from exercising—and strengthening—these essential muscles. Randy realized that in order to support her daughter, she needed to learn to sit with this intolerably painful anxiety and *not* act on it (or react to it). She realized that learning to tolerate and manage her own anxiety would ultimately help her daughter.

"I don't know how to do this," Randy said in a discouraged tone.

I suggested that she likely *had* done this before, earlier in Ellen's development, and she could use this as a reference point. "Like when she was learning to walk," I said. "I know that this was a long time ago, but can you recall how you felt then?"

"Oh, yes," Randy said, lighting up. "It was such an exciting and sweet time. I remember watching her hold on to the coffee table, steady herself, and try to walk. Even if she'd fall, she'd look over at me, get up, and try again."

She paused and thought about her role at that time.

"Let me think . . . how did I do it? It didn't seem hard at the time. I intuitively knew that I couldn't hold her up, move her legs for her, or pick her up each time she fell. But I was there for her. Supporting her emotionally. Cheering her on, trusting that her body would learn from her falls and improve through its wobbly practice. I remembered what a thrill it was to watch her revel in *her* excitement about her new-found ability!"

"And while the stakes may seem higher now," I said, "the process will follow a similar pattern."

Randy smiled as she took this in.

We cannot bypass the essential internal process that happens as we develop confidence and mastery of new skills. This process is essential to intrinsic motivation! We, as parents, cannot master these skills for our kids. We cannot sculpt them in this way.

Ellen's mastery of these skills will become the building blocks of her growth.

BREAKING THE CYCLE

In order to disrupt the anxiety spiral and have a breakthrough with our kids, we first need to become aware of our own parenting anxieties and thought distortions.

Common Sculptor Thought Distortions:

- Catastrophizing: Randy feared that if Ellen didn't improve, she would never live independently and "live in her basement."
- Overgeneralizing: Randy was convinced that all (ital) teens Ellen's age were capable and self directed.
- Labeling: Ellen internalized Randy's accusations of being lazy and unmotivated which didn't address the source - her debilitating anxiety.

If Randy had never realized that it was her response to anxiety that caused her to pressure Ellen (therefore causing Ellen to freeze up), she never would have been able to break the cycle.

It's hard to break habits and behavioral patterns. It makes us anxious. So it's doubly important that we become aware of our own anxious tendencies so we can learn how to interrupt them in the moment.

A Sculptor who is determined to break this cycle cannot do so through strength of will alone. They must learn to replace their old habits with new ones to support their teen's growth.

Once Randy became aware of her anxiety process, she slowed down and listened to—and responded to—Ellen differently. Rather than coming up with a solution, she began to ask Ellen, "What do you need from me? What would be helpful?"

Ellen responded: "I need you to slow down. Follow my lead and go at my pace. Focus on *my* process, not the outcome!"

As Randy reassured Ellen that she would not accelerate or interfere, Ellen was less inclined to resist advancement. Ellen felt less self-conscious and anxious about exploring when she was allowed to do it at her own pace.

With this pressure alleviated, Ellen slowly began to access and report desires, interests, curiosities.

FREE AT LAST, ELLEN CREATES HERSELF

Only after letting go of the need to sculpt did the vision for what Ellen might become begin to appear.

With this shift in the dynamic, Ellen began expressing more interest in peer relationships, particularly with friends she had made at school. To get together with friends who lived outside of the city, she needed to transport herself independently—to drive. Although she had her license and understood the mechanics of driving, she had had minimal experience and lacked the confidence to drive herself. This became an identified goal: the literal and figurative vehicle to revising her relationship with her mother.

Ellen wanted and needed Randy's help to gain experience and confidence while driving, but in order to make this a productive exercise, both of them needed to learn to own and manage their respective anxieties.

Ellen asked Randy to accompany her and provide specific instructions that would help to improve her driving skills, but not enable her feeling of dependence. Ellen was aware that her anxiety was likely to rise when she was in the car, leading to the temptation to fall back into the familiar pattern of getting Randy to do it for her. So, prior to their practice driving sessions, they planned accordingly, each committing to a new role.

For example, if Ellen became anxious while driving and asked her mother if it was okay to switch lanes, they agreed that Randy would say "You've checked the rearview and the side mirrors, and there are no cars coming." Instead of Randy checking for her, Randy would simply assure Ellen that she was capably taking the appropriate steps. Randy reinforced that Ellen's instincts were reliable and trustworthy.

Additionally, Randy had to resist the urge to direct Ellen, either through offering unsolicited suggestions or by reactively grabbing the wheel. Such behaviors would inadvertently create roadblocks to Ellen's independence. Ellen needed to learn to trust her own internal judgments rather than relying on Randy's direction.

It is in resisting these urges to direct, to sculpt, that the breakthrough occurred for Randy.

Each time Randy's anxiety tempted her to offer unsolicited advice or commands or to reach for the steering wheel, she paused and internally walked herself through the following steps:

- She acknowledged her "roadblock"—her anxiety around Ellen's discomfort.
- She empathized with Ellen's anxiety.
- She reminded herself of her intention to be supportive.
- She respected Ellen's pace and process.
- She asked Ellen how she could be of help.

As their work together progressed, Ellen dictated the pace, slowly becoming a less passive, more active participant in her own life. She gained access to what she wanted, and displayed ownership, curiosity, and hopefulness.

From this point on, Ellen defined ways that Randy could respond to her more helpfully. This was especially important, because for the first time Ellen was taking agency, able to identify her anxiety and specify the ways of soothing it. Randy was not the problem-solver, but the respondent to Ellen's direction.

Each week, they drove together and reported the improvements. Gradually Randy removed herself from the car and Ellen felt confident enough to drive on her own. This was exciting and refreshing for both of them!

Eventually, we began to apply this experience to other independent activities. As we discussed Ellen's challenges of looking for work, each time Randy interrupted, offering strategies and connections for work, we humorously reminded her of her backseat driving! Because of Randy's experience of seeing Ellen's progress in driving the car, she readily accepted the metaphor and playfully assumed the role Ellen assigned, be it copilot, guest, backseat driver, or silent passenger.

As the school year progressed, Ellen began babysitting a nine-year-old boy in their building. Ellen enjoyed her developing relationship with this boy and appreciated the parents' reliance on her. She often "rescued" them from unexpected coverage dilemmas, and this role was empowering and satisfying for Ellen. Ellen developed a fondness for the family and a connection to the child's mother. As the relationship evolved, the mother shared details of her work as a nurse practitioner, which piqued Ellen's interest, particularly given her comfort level with science.

With this new adult role model's encouragement, Ellen researched programs and enrolled in prerequisite classes to apply for this degree. Finally in the driver's seat, Ellen was able to pave her road toward independence.

OVERCOMING THE SCULPTOR'S ANXIETY

On some level, we're all Sculptors. Every parent has a vision of raising a kid who's going to flourish in their own way. If you saw yourself reflected in Randy's story, congratulations—you've achieved another level of self-awareness! If you identified with the Sculptor's anxiety, that's great. We've got a roadmap for how to manage that anxiety and move forward:

- The first step is to realize that you have anxiety. You're human; of course you do! But your anxiety manifests as a drive to overcome imperfections and shape the world, and your kid(s), according to your vision. Identifying these tendencies as anxiety is key.
- The second step is to reestablish your goal: Your goal is to create a flourishing person who develops their own internal skills. Part of making our kids functioning, competent people is to allow them the experience of being an expert.
- The third step is to recognize that your anxiety is a barrier to achieving that goal. If you focus so much on sculpting your child that you take away their agency and ability to do things on their own, you are robbing them of this experience, of seeing themselves as experts.
- The fourth step is to allow your child to take the lead. Respect their process, go at their pace, and give them permission to tell you how to be a support.
- Resist the urge of believing that you know best, and let your child tell you what they need from you.
- Let your child exercise the muscles you've been unwittingly preventing them from using. You need to allow your child to have

agency in order for them to develop the skills, the lack of which are causing you anxiety in the first place!

Randy experienced firsthand the benefits of following these steps. Ellen became an expert on herself! And because of Randy's willingness to follow Ellen's lead, Randy got to learn how to best support Ellen, and she became an expert at managing her own anxieties along the way.

Chapter 5

Stacey the Game
Show Contestant

I first met Stacey four months after the birth of her son, Steven. The week prior, Stacey had taken herself to the emergency room with chest pains, heart palpitations, and breathlessness, certain that she was having a heart attack. After many tests and consultations, she was diagnosed as having had a panic attack and discharged with a referral for therapy.

In the waiting room, I was greeted by a tall, striking, thirty-six-year-old woman. She had long straight brown hair, dark eyes, and a precisely outlined, red-lipstick smile. Dressed in a crisp white button-down shirt, fitted jeans, and low-heeled boots, she did not have the frazzled, formula-stained, elastic-waisted-comfort-wear look that I associated with my own early months of motherhood.

As she sat on the office couch, she readily volunteered a detailed account of her panic attack. Coming from "out of the blue," it had been a scary and destabilizing experience, one that had shaken her to her core.

Stacey asked many questions about the mechanics of panic attacks and sought a factual understanding of its physiology. She clearly found solace in acquiring as much concrete information as she could. She was eager to develop techniques to prevent and manage future attacks, should they occur, so we agreed to meet regularly to do so.

Over the next couple of months, as Stacey acquired an understanding of her brain's responses to anxiety and its corresponding effect on her body, she also began to explore the causes of her anxiety. Time and time again what would come up was her unexpected, growing indecision about returning to work.

She had already created a carefully devised working-motherhood plan. The resistance she was feeling around returning to work threatened to derail her plans, so she chose to avoid these feelings. Essentially, her indecision was causing her anxiety!

She had always thought that working was the "right" decision for her and her family, and she was loathe to reconsider this choice. She was reluctant to acknowledge her resistance for fear that it would open a complicated and unwelcome Pandora's box of anxiety-producing thoughts—most significantly, the prospect that she had made the "wrong" choice about being a working mother.

WHO ARE GAME SHOW CONTESTANT PARENTS?

The game show *Let's Make a Deal* originated in the United States in 1963, and as of 2022, is still running. The structure of the game is simple: Contestants are awarded a prize of medium value, say, $1,000. Then they are offered a choice—they can keep their initial prize, or they can trade it for a mystery prize behind a curtain. The mystery item could be something of great value, like a car, or a prank prize (called Zonks), like a gigantic pair of pants. The contestant is placed in the position of needing to make a decision. Will they keep what they have or risk it for the chance of something greater?

The nature of *Let's Make a Deal* highlights the inherent anxiety that takes place when any of us are confronted with a decision. Because the mystery prize is unknown, there is no way of knowing if we're making the right decision or not! The contestant's anxiety arises when presented with the need to make these decisions. Stuck in not knowing what the right choice is, they are paralyzed with anxiety, afraid of making the wrong move.

Such was Stacey's dilemma.

She and her husband had meticulously crafted their family plan. She chose the "right" time to become parents, in accordance with her career trajectory. Her work was an integral part of her identity, and she was certain that she would return to her job after becoming a mother. She had strategically arranged twenty weeks of maternity leave, and had already hired a highly qualified nanny in anticipation of her return to the workplace.

She had agreed to participate in her game show knowing in advance what decision she would make. She was going to keep the first prize and not risk it all on what might be behind the curtain. But now, faced with the prospect of actually returning to work, she was full of doubts. She just couldn't make a decision!

Doubt and uncertainty are debilitating for Game Show Contestants (GSCs), precisely because they pride themselves on their good judgment and decisiveness. Stacey's team at work, especially her magazine's editor in chief, valued and relied on her excellent decision-making and judgment, and on her keen aesthetic eye. Used to being in control and knowing what to do, GSCs like Stacey crumble when faced with indecision and uncertainty.

Game Show Contestant Perks:

- Highly Rational: GSC parents use reasoning and logic to solve problems. Because they are methodical and logical, others appreciate their reliability and predictability.
- Decisive: Given their ability to distill complex problems into simplified categories, they're confident decision makers and relied on others to do so.
- Achieve Goals: Once the GSC has chosen their door, they follow through to completion. They remain focused on their perceived "right" goal and they stay on track—other doors are no longer available to them.

WHAT'S BEHIND DOOR #2?

Ultimately, Stacey began to accept and tolerate the coexistence of her seemingly conflicting feelings. She realized that working motherhood was an ongoing process that she would continue to evaluate as she progressed; she could change her mind, if she wanted, and find alternative creative solutions. With her husband's understanding and support, the validation she found in our sessions, and a deepened understanding of her anxiety, she returned to work with more ease and self-acceptance.

A decade or so had passed when Stacey resurfaced. In her inimitably humorous and likable way, she left a message on my voicemail.

"I'm baaaack," she said in a singsong voice. "Same church, different pew! I'm freaking out about Steven's high school decision!"

I returned her call and we made an appointment.

Even though she was now in her mid-forties and the mother of two preteens, Stacey looked as if she hadn't aged a bit since our initial meeting so many years ago.

"What's going on?" I asked.

Referring to her dilemma as "an embarrassment of riches," she explained.

After engaging in the cutthroat application process of New York City public and private high schools, her son had received acceptances from both his first-choice private school and his top-rated public school. Yet, as the commitment deadline approached, Stacey found, once again, that she could not act. She found herself overcome with indecision about which school was right for her son. Fearful that he'd lose a coveted spot entirely, and desperate for relief, Stacey and her husband placed a nonrefundable deposit at the private school *and* enrolled him in the public high school. Within days, this temporary relief had transformed into obsessive panic.

"Don't judge me. I know this might not be fair, and we *will* pull the trigger soon, but we needed to buy a little time—literally. We are leaning toward public school, but it just doesn't sit well. I can't decide what's right!"

Like many privileged New York City families, Stacey and her husband Andrew had long been proponents of public education. Yet, given the uncertainty of the Department of Education's high-school matching system, their son was not guaranteed a seat at one of the schools for which they believed he was best suited. Thus, they mitigated the uncertainty by applying to private schools as a backup option, "Just to be safe."

Now, with his simultaneous acceptances in hand, she felt less confident about the planned public-school option. Her uncertainty about the decision propelled her into a GSC anxiety spiral, including the anxious thought traps (cognitive distortions) of black-and-white thinking and catastrophizing.

"Obviously, public school makes the most sense," Stacey said. "But every time I think about it, I get a pit in my stomach. Like I'm cutting corners at *the most important* time of his educational career. Once you've seen the offerings of the private school, the public school cannot compare! This is such an important time in his development, and the individualized attention, the opportunities, and the facilities at the private school are unbelievable. If we can afford it, then we *should* enroll him there, right?"

She paused for a moment before continuing.

"Yet, if we send him to private, we must send our daughter to private. We will have paid hundreds of thousands of dollars before they even go to college. Is it really worth it? Is the quality of the education *that* much better? In the scheme of things, does a nice campus *really* matter? On the other hand, are we squandering an amazing opportunity for him because of money? Isn't this the best use of our hard-earned money? But both Andrew and I went to public school, and we have done well!"

As she shared her dilemma, she became observably anxious. Her speech accelerated and she became physically tense, with a pained look on her face. Terrified of making a parental mistake and steering her teen in the "wrong" direction, she wavered between the options. And the more she vacillated, the wider she cast her net of indecision:

"Maybe we should sell our apartment and buy a house in the suburbs. Maybe we could have avoided this process altogether? It seems kind of late to disrupt our entire living situation to answer an education decision. Besides, who's to say that this would be a good solution for any of us?"

She clearly felt desperate, and, as she claimed, was even more overwhelmed with anxiety than she had been at our first meeting. "I barely recognize myself," she said. "But now the stakes are so much higher!"

THE GSC'S DILEMMA

Parenting is a high-pressure undertaking, replete with responsibilities and the need to make important decisions on behalf of our children. Particularly when achievement is in the mix, parents may convince themselves that decisions are as binary as choosing the correct prize in a game show, where one has an empirically higher value than the other: Is this the right teacher? Did I steer my child in the wrong direction by enrolling him in this program? Is this the right environment for her?

Many friends have counseled me as I've deliberated over parenting decisions, big and small. And nearly every day in my office, a parent asks, Is that the right thing to say? or What's the right way to handle this? or Was it wrong to do that? Was I right to push him about this? Was I wrong to make her stay home and study? Did I emphasize the right activities? Was this the right fit? Was I wrong to encourage the more advanced program?

The trap that GSC parents fall into is believing that a single decision will make or break their future (or their child's future). For example, she must take biology this year, or it will derail her science trajectory for the remainder of high school, which will dilute the strength of her college application and jeopardize her acceptance to a *good* school, which will place her future success at risk. This approach channels their anxieties into the decisions themselves.

This style manifests in opposite sides of the same coin: indecisiveness or decisiveness. GSCs may ruminate over options, and obsessively review or second-guess their decision once they've made it. Conversely, they may approach situations in an overly rational, cut-and-dried manner that denies nuance: This school is good, this school is bad. One succeeds, or one fails.

Either way, such parents believe that certainty exists and a successful future hinges on their ability to always pick the correct path.

WHEN A DECISION ISN'T JUST A DECISION

The scale of Stacey's anxiety was reflective of the decision's symbolic significance and its unique unconscious meaning to her. This seemingly simple decision between public school vs. private school had a more complex, psychological import to her psyche.

If you see yourself in Stacey's story, take heed. Often when we find ourselves making a mountain out of a molehill (e.g., thinking the choice of high school is the be-all and end-all of our child's future), it's because we're unconsciously linking this particular molehill to a traumatic experience in our past.

I assured Stacey that we would methodically examine this difficult decision together, but to do so, we needed to soothe and calm her activated anxiety system.

"Rather than criticizing the feelings of doubt and indecision," I said, "let's acknowledge them and allow their presence. It takes more energy to resist the feeling than to accept it. That doesn't mean that you need to like it or welcome it. But resisting feelings triggers a whole host of physiological responses. Ultimately resisting anxious feelings makes us more anxious, and the cycle continues until we can't hold it in anymore and voila—anxiety attack."

"Yes, I remember we talked about that," Stacey said. "That's what I tell my kids when their anxiety alarm systems sound. But it's so hard to apply that knowledge to myself!"

"I agree," I replied. "It's one of the beauties of being a therapist—I can't always apply this to myself, but I can always advise others on the process!"

We took a moment to physiologically slow her body down. Placing our feet firmly on the floor and our hands on our knees, we inhaled slowly and exhaled slowly, together. This co-regulation conveyed messages of safety and grounding to her brain's anxious protection center.

From a calmer, less physiologically agitated state, she considered that her heightened response was likely to contain vestiges of traumas and anxieties from her past. I wondered aloud if she had any associations from her own history, particularly her adolescence.

STACEY'S STORY

With thoughtful reflection, Stacey reminded me that her parents had emigrated from Iran to the United States to escape sociopolitical unrest and to complete their medical training. As they began their careers, they settled in an affluent California suburb, where they raised their growing family, Stacey and her younger brothers.

While her parents achieved great financial and professional success in this country, her mother's mental health suffered greatly. "She is a very difficult and harsh person," said Stacey. "We've had a rocky relationship for as long as I can remember." According to Stacey, while her mother's moods had always been unpredictable, she became especially volatile as Stacey approached adolescence. Rather than allowing her more privileges, Stacey's mother tightened her parental reins, monitoring what Stacey was allowed to wear, weighing in on Stacey's grades, her studying, and her social life. As a compliant and responsible teen, Stacey attributed her mother's rigidity to the stresses of immigration and traumas that she had likely endured in Iran, but never shared with her children.

Her mother's immigration cast a shadow over Stacey's upbringing. Her childhood was replete with both gratitude and guilt. She knew how much her parents had sacrificed and risked by moving to the United States, with the intention of providing themselves and ultimately their children with a "better life," with more freedom.

Her mother may have physically left the Middle East, but her emotions about her past life were ever present. She was chronically fearful, stressed, and unhappy. Stacey explained, "Everything was always everyone else's fault. She blamed her anger, her sadness, her frustrations, on us. And because I was the oldest, I felt the most responsible." In her mind, Stacey connected her mother's misery to their fateful decision to move to the United States. She often wondered what would have happened if her family had chosen to stay in Iran. Would her mother have been better off? She had come for a better life, but how much better was this life for her, when she was so unhappy here.

UNDERSTANDING THE GSC'S ANXIETY

GSC anxiety is built around the idea that personal success or failure (for them or their kids) hinges on certain critical decision points.

For the record, it doesn't. Life is a complicated maze. A myriad of decisions, of potential nexus points, that influence our future paths. Believing that any decision can make or break the future is a classic example of black-and-white thinking. As in, one path is right, and the other is wrong. One future is bright, and the other is dark.

Stacey was raised in a family with a dual nature, one that lent itself to black-and-white thinking: new country / old country, good country/ bad country, right way of being and acting/wrong way of being and acting, and so forth. This is not to say there aren't big decisions that will have an outsized influence on the future; it's just that these decisions are not as binary as good choice / bad choice. GSCs get trapped into believing there is a definitively right and wrong way to live life and to make choices.

Game Show anxiety is triggered by:

- Indecisiveness: Not knowing which decision is the "right" one to make is the major catalyst for this PART's anxiety spirals.
- Ambiguity and Doubt:The GSC prefers "knowing" and has minimal tolerance for nuance. They become anxious when they can't employ reason or logic to emotionally laden issues. Even a little doubt can be paralyzing for a GSC. This PART is so used to feeling self-assured and confident that feelings of doubt can set off existential and even identity crises.

The GSC manages anxiety by:

- being extremely rational and methodical about their decision-making process.
- In day-to-day life they make decisions easily and confidently. Many decisions are no-brainers because they fit easily into categories of "the right way" or "the wrong way" to do something. GSCs have strong value systems and feel confident in knowing themselves and what they want out of life.

For GSCs, making the right decisions is a highly valued skill. That's why doubt and indecision are such major triggers for them. They are accustomed to knowing what the "right" choice is, and believe strongly that if they make the wrong choice, the consequences will be disastrous.

All of this was true for Stacey.

Up until the panic attack that had brought her to my office the first time, Stacey's life had progressed at a pace and cadence that she liked. She attributed this to her good decision-making: She chose a career that she liked and excelled in; she chose a partner; she chose to get married; and she "chose" to become pregnant—all at times and at a pace that she had decided on. She did not overthink, worry, or regret her decisions once she had made them. She made decisions and moved on.

Her family, friends, and colleagues trusted her judgment. She had every reason to believe she had cracked the code. So, when she was initially confronted with the indecision of whether or not to return to work after giving birth, it was catastrophe for her. It was not so much the decision itself that triggered her anxiety, but the indecision and doubt about what the right thing to do was. Similarly, it was her doubt about her son's high school decision that brought her back to my office.

THE ANXIETY SPIRAL

For Stacey, adolescence was the beginning of the end of the healthy relationship she had had with her mom. One of her greatest fears was that she would somehow repeat this pattern with her son—that by making the wrong decision, she would somehow ruin her son's life and her son would blame her for his unhappiness.

Unconsciously, she placed the weight of her fears on the decision of what high school her son should go to. No wonder she was so anxious about deciding! But it was, in fact, the act of not deciding that was putting strain on their relationship.

Stacey wanted to give her son the freedom to decide, but Steven genuinely liked both schools. Sure, he was slightly more attracted to the private school because of all the bells and whistles, but he also liked the public-school option, and he was uncomfortable asking his parents to take on the additional financial burden for a school that he liked only slightly better. He was only thirteen, and he needed his parents to help make the decision, but they were not doing so.

Not knowing where he was going to go to school was causing its own discomfort. All of his friends knew where they were going. They were talking and daydreaming about what they were going to do at their new school and making the kind of loose plans for the future that thirteen-year-olds make. Steven, meanwhile, was left out of these conversations, stuck in not-knowing, and creating his own anxious associations with the process of decision-making.

THE ANXIETY GAME

What parents become fixated on is emblematic of their anxiety. Stacey became fixated on these perceived "nexus" decisions because that's what she was anxious about.

In general, parental anxiety is heightened because it's a protective mechanism, and the parental need to protect is already super heightened. Parents feel a need to protect themselves, protect their kids, and protect themselves from seeing their kids in pain. They become so fixated on managing their anxiety and the things they are anxious about that they lose sight of what their actual goals are. In Stacey's case, she became so fixated on the school dilemma that she lost sight of what Steven needed.

Parents are supposed to provide a stable base for their kids, a foundation upon which their kids can grow. In giving in to her indecision, Stacey was unintentionally creating an environment that was unstable. Her son felt untethered. He needed his parents in this moment to provide direction and stability, and they couldn't provide that. It's anxiety-producing for kids to see their parents paralyzed by anxiety.

There are also many benefits to kids seeing parents work through their decision-making process, benefits that were being withheld by Stacey not engaging in the process. In every way, the act of not making a decision was more detrimental than the possible risks of making the so-called "wrong" choice.

It's entirely possible that if this continued much longer, Steven would learn to withhold information or avoid sharing decisions with his mom in order to avoid a repeat of this kind of behavior.

Common Game Show Contestant pitfalls:

- The GSC's rarely "think outside of the box" and narrow their options where more may exist.
- Inhibits creative problem-solving: Stacey's anxiety was so "loud" that it prevented her from taking a step back and thinking through the dilemma more flexibly. She never stopped to ask herself, "What will happen if he doesn't like the school we select? What could we do? Maybe there's value in trying something out and seeing how it works?" The possibility of her son reapplying to the other school if he was unhappy with the initial decision never occurred to her.
- Emphasize outcomes over process: GSC often underestimate the value and learning and growth which happens during the decision-making process.

- Intentions and values get lost: This would have been (and ultimately was) a great "teachable" moment. For example, she could have explained *how* they were approaching the decision, such as: "What's most important to us is that you are exposed to new ways of thinking and learning and that you begin to discover what 'lights you up'—what subjects you like, what kind of person you want to be, etc. We want a school where you can find peers you like and teachers who inspire you. We want a school where you feel safe to explore, both emotionally and physically. We are trying to determine which school is more likely to offer this, and we are basing our decision on these values."
- They could have asked Steven, "What's most important to you in a school?" By asking him, Stacey would have demonstrated respect for his developmental stage by offering him agency and collaboration, and given him the chance to formulate his own ideas.
- Attributes unhappiness and anxiety to a decision: Stacey is so focused on "the decision" that she thinks *the school* is the determining factor of whether or not Steven will be happy. Because of this, she is not appreciating that *how* her son interacts with school will be a greater determinant of his happiness/success than *the school* itself. If, for example, her son was to become depressed during the school year, it may not be attributable to the school at all. There are many contributing factors to mental health, and it is rare that one factor alone (like school) is the sole cause. By focusing solely on the decision, Stacey was at risk of losing sight of the whole of her son's life.

FACING THE ANXIETY

During our sessions, as Stacey began to understand the generational nature of her anxiety and how it distorted her way of thinking, she became more capable of comparing and contrasting what had happened in her past with what was happening in her present. In other words, she was able to see the vast differences between her upbringing and the way that she was raising her children.

Stacey realized she had conflated her parents' decision to emigrate with her son's high-school dilemma. The major difference: reversibility.

Unlike the permanence of her parents' immigration decision, the school decision was not irreversible. Though school systems have strict parameters, if her son attended public school and found that it didn't suit him well, he would be able to reapply to private school.

Stacey grew up in an environment where major decisions were irreversible and learned to think of all decisions in that context; hence, her panic when faced with Door #2. In reality, her son's high-school decision, like most big choices in life, wasn't the end. It was a starting point for the next chapter in his development. High school is not a time for irreversible decisions. As a developmental phase, it is particularly dynamic and fluid.

BREAKING THE CYCLE

Through several exercises, Stacey was able to clarify and verbalize her core values, particularly regarding education. She valued education that would promote her son's *holistic* growth—his ability to learn, develop new skills, mature, and stay stimulated and engaged. She admitted that both schools seemed to meet those needs.

As she honed these values, she articulated them to Steven, modeling the thought process that was driving and informing her decision. She explained to him, "It's not just that we 'want you to be happy.' We also want you to enjoy learning, find peers that you relate to, and feel like you're stimulated and interested. If you pick a school and feel like this is not happening, we can always reconsider."

Ultimately, they decided on public school. It matched all of their core values and was a decision that Stacey, her husband, and Steven all felt comfortable with. Importantly, Stacey also encouraged ongoing discussion with her son about what his experience of school was. She not only opened the lines of communication with him when making the decision, but kept them open afterwards, expressing interest and respect for Steven's perspectives.

Common Thought Distortions:

- Black and White Thinking: Of all the types, GSC's are the most prone to dichotomous thinking. Stacey believed that a there was a "right" and a "wrong" decision and that a school's quality could be reduced to "good" or "bad"

- Magnification: While this was undoubtedly an important decision, its exaggerated significance paralyzed Stacey. She believed that her son's entire educational trajectory rested on this decision.

OVERCOMING THE GAME SHOW CONTESTANT'S ANXIETY

Everyone can relate to the need to "get it right," but when that need becomes so great that we're paralyzed and afraid to take action, that's a good indication that we're in the clutches of GSC anxiety.

The first step to overcoming this anxiety is, as always, to recognize that we're having an anxious response. When we're in the clutches of anxiety it's nearly impossible to think logically and use our higher-level brain functions. In order to think critically, we need to allow the anxiety to pass through us. Once we realize we're having an anxious response, we can take a moment, breathe, and break our anxious spiral so we can return to our decision-making process with clear eyes and a fresh perspective.

There are several tools we can use to help ground us in reality and break our spiral:

- **Recognizing thought distortions:** Our anxieties disrupt reality. This contributes to our not being able to see a situation clearly or objectively. If we can identify these distortions, we can say, "That's my anxiety talking! This is an anxiety-fueled thought that is not a fact—it's a fear."
- **Differentiating past from present:** Stacey was paralyzed with anxiety because she equated her son's high-school decision with her parents' decision to emigrate to the United States. But these scenarios were not the same. Her son's high-school decision was reversible, whereas her parents' decision to emigrate was not. Once she was able to separate these scenarios in her mind, she was able to see her son's high-school decision much more clearly.
- **Playing out the worst-case scenario:** GSCs are frequent victims of catastrophic thinking. They believe that making the wrong

decision will bring the world down around them. This fear can be allayed by actually considering the worst-case scenario. In Steven's case, the worst-case scenario wound up being that he would transfer schools. In Stacey's mind she was afraid that choosing the wrong school would ruin her relationship with her son forever, but the reality, when she considered it, was much less bleak.

- **Acknowledging the validity of indecision:** Stacey was afraid of making the wrong decision, but in reality, both options available to her were good options. Steven genuinely liked both schools. While Stacey was paralyzed and afraid of making the decision, the reason for it was a positive one. She had two *good* options. And when you have two good options, it can be hard to choose. Acknowledging that the perfect answer did not exist and that there were clear upsides and advantages to either decision helped Stacey become much more comfortable with her indecision.

After a year of public school, and some discussion, Steven wound up reapplying and transferring to private school.

This reinforced for Stacey, and everyone involved, that these decisions are not irreversible. Adolescence is a time of trial and error; ultimately this school trial was valuable to the whole family, and taught Stacey and her son a great deal about the process of decision-making.

The emotional opportunities that this experience offered were, ultimately, more valuable than the opportunities she was initially considering regarding Steven's education.

Chapter 6

Alice the Crowd-Pleaser

Alice sought treatment in her late forties to help manage feelings of stress which had been intensifying over the past year. A married, working mother of two teenage daughters, she was experiencing age-related medical issues, marital conflict, and was caring for her elderly father, whose health was deteriorating. No wonder she was feeling stressed!

Most patients come to their sessions in casual clothes, but Alice always showed up dressed to the nines, featuring up-to-the-minute trends. Even her casual wear was fully accessorized and reflected the latest styles. A well-known event planner, she was notorious for her cleverly themed parties and unmatched aesthetic. Appropriately, she loved everything about a good party—the planning, the organizing, the executing. A self-proclaimed extrovert, Alice had been the social chair of her college sorority and had maintained versions of "the social organizer" role throughout her adulthood. She was a hostess extraordinaire. Her peers sought her input and taste on issues ranging from fashion to home decor and, of course, party planning.

Yet, despite her many strengths and obvious privilege, she was plagued by nagging sadness and chronic nervousness, and she was guilt-ridden about the way she behaved toward her husband and daughters. Over the years, she had become more and more critical of her family, irritable and impatient, bickering with them and creating overall tension in her home. She couldn't put her finger on why but knew she had to get a handle on it, and so she came to me.

WHO ARE CROWD-PLEASERS?

Of all the different PARTs, that of the Crowd-Pleaser seems most common. As social creatures we humans often struggle to figure out how we as individuals fit into the various groups we're a part of. How do we guarantee our belonging, and with whom? The anxiety of the Crowd-Pleaser taps into the essential human necessity of needing to belong.

Crowd-Pleasers are driven by unconscious (or sometimes conscious) fears of humiliation, abandonment, or being ostracized (#cancel-culture!). These fears inform their thought processes and motivate self-protective behaviors. Crowd-Pleasers are hooked into the cultural norms, know the latest and greatest styles, and quickly adjust to and internalize community trends. They are rarely "left out" as they ensure that they are providing what is needed by their peers and their communities in order to be part of the in-group.

As parents they feel it is their duty to make sure their kids are never left out and are always keeping up with their peers. Essentially, it is the desire for social acceptance and belonging for themselves and their children that defines the Crowd-Pleaser.

Crowd Pleaser Perks:

- Trendsetters: Due to their attunement to the cultural trends, Crowd-Pleasers can be on the cutting edge and introduce their peers to the latest and greatest.
- Social Organizers: Crowd-Pleasers value group activities and engagement.They are team players and can coordinate gatherings; they stay relevant and current.
- Maintain High Standards: Crowd-Pleasers strive for excellence to fit in and to stand out; they use their competitive urges to improve and they often raise the aspirational bar within the crowd.

Crowd-Pleasers are both highly competitive and conscious of how they fit into the social landscape. They want to be ahead of the curve but not outliers. They stay aware of the "competition" and often view their current family, or family of origin, as the foundation upon which they base their perceptions and behaviors. They use others as their baseline and predominant point of reference for what they and their kids should be achieving.

ALICE'S STORY

Alice was the only daughter and youngest of her parents' four children. As a toddler, she was diagnosed with an unusual genetic condition (mild hemihyperplasia), in which parts of one side of her body grew asymmetrically, impacting her appearance. Her right eye was nearly closed (a "lazy eye"), and her right leg and arm were significantly shorter than those on her left. Throughout her childhood, her mother brought her to many medical specialists and had her undergo a series of treatments and surgeries to "correct these abnormalities."

Alice described her mother as a beautiful and vain woman who placed great import on her own appearance. Thus, Alice's physical "imperfections" held particular significance and created distress for her mother. Alice recalls that her mother dressed her in the finest of clothes, spending time and money shopping and curating her wardrobe. Alice interpreted this as both her mother's expression of love and as a way to compensate for Alice's physical imperfection.

From this early age, Alice, like so many of us, learned that she needed to appear a certain way to others in order to fit in. Alice explicitly describes her narrative as a classic "ugly duckling" story. She claimed that through a combination of puberty and many corrective and cosmetic procedures, she experienced a pivotal transformation in her appearance, from an awkward and "defective" girl to an attractive teen who received considerable attention. She enjoyed social popularity and attention from boys. She cherished this newfound admiration, particularly in contrast to the way she had previously perceived herself.

Unsurprisingly, her appearance became deeply intertwined with her identity and self-worth. Her predominant mechanism for self-acceptance seemed to be acceptance from others. Without it, she felt deeply flawed and imperfect. Psychologically (and largely unconsciously) her appearance became a way to manage insecurities and anxieties. Focusing on and "improving" her appearance was her go-to method for improving her deep-seated feelings of inadequacy and unacceptability. This emphasis on visual detail helped her succeed in life, namely in her profession. It transcended self-worth and became the vehicle for Alice's career and material success as well.

Additionally, keeping up appearances was deeply embedded in her family culture. Her father, the owner of a fabric manufacturing company, took great pride in his acquired affluence. Described as a "bon vivant," he enjoyed the material pleasures that accompanied his wealth—an expensive wine collection, his country club membership, and lavish European travel. Similarly, he enjoyed the image that his lifestyle portrayed to his community.

Unfortunately, and through a questionable turn of events, he lost his fortune during Alice's late adolescence. Forced to modify their lifestyle, they sold the family home, ceased their club memberships and travel, and assumed a more modest standard of living. This downgrade was a source of deep shame for her father and catalyzed a depression from which he never recovered. Her mother masterfully maintained the appearance of wealth, despite this devastating financial upset, working part-time in a women's boutique to style others and thus receive discounts on items for her own wardrobe.

The lesson Alice took away from all of this: Appearances are everything.

Once Alice became a mother, her social circle expanded as she socialized and organized gatherings for parents in her community. Naturally, she assumed a heightened social awareness with her daughters as well. She was a valued and integral part of the community and expected that her daughters would follow suit.

Alice had her finger on the pulse of not only fashion and party trends, but academics as well. Through her social circles and connections, she was kept apprised of the most sought-after schools. Not surprisingly, she knew the standing and ranking of most of her daughters' classmates, and she strategized with a well-connected college counselor to increase the likelihood of her daughters' early acceptance to Ivy League schools.

THE CROWD-PLEASER'S DILEMMA

Crowd-Pleasers were taught as children that social acceptance was one of the most important—if not *the* most important—part of life. And this is arguably true. Social belonging is a standard metric when measuring quality of life. We all need it, to some degree, in order to be happy.

But there are many kinds of social belonging. This may be hard to believe, in a world where the number of social media followers one has is a standard measure of success, but the healthiest social bonds are often not with large groups of acquaintances or strangers. Social belonging, as it correlates to personal happiness, is a sense of relatedness connected to positive, lasting, and significant interpersonal relationships.

The age-old adage "You can't please everyone" is, unfortunately for Crowd-Pleasers, very true. Alice discovered, much to her disquiet, that her efforts to keep up appearances were creating an anxious and stressful home life for her and her family. Alice came to realize that she was sacrificing the health and well-being of herself and her family in order to achieve the acceptance of others—her key measure of success.

It was ultimately Alice's Crowd-Pleaser anxiety that prevented her from being there for her daughter Carly when she needed her mother the most.

KEEP-UP CARLY

Carly was certainly her mother's daughter. She was status-conscious, in beauty, fashion, and academics. She maintained a high academic and social standing, and Alice did everything in her power to ensure that Carly stayed at the front of the curve. If Carly's grades were at risk of slipping, Alice paid for and arranged sessions with the most coveted and specialized tutors for support. Carly met with a tutor several times per week throughout her junior year for college standardized test prep.

As Carly's senior year approached, she spent hours writing her college application essay, collating her extracurricular experiences and her stellar grades for an early decision application. This was the culmination of years of planning and strategizing. Being accepted into an Ivy League school had been her declared life's purpose since middle school. She maintained a nearly perfect GPA, and after taking the ACT test many times, she eventually received the score she had aspired to reach. Carly was hopeful that she had played her cards right and had made herself a viable candidate for her first-choice school.

Unfortunately, several weeks into her senior year, a crisis emerged.

Alice was contacted by a representative from the ACT testing company. The company was questioning the credibility and accuracy of her daughter's scores. Due to Carly's significant point increase and the striking resemblance of her answers to those of a classmate who was seated nearby during the test, the system had flagged her results.

Carly fervently denied any wrongdoing or cheating, and, according to the company's policy, they did not intend to notify Carly's school of this misalignment. Nonetheless, the accusation threw Alice into an anxiety tailspin. Flooded with memories of her father's financial downturn during her late adolescence, she anticipated public humiliation, shame, loss of status—a Crowd-Pleaser's worst nightmare.

UNDERSTANDING THE
CROWD-PLEASER'S ANXIETY

A Crowd-Pleaser's sense of self-worth is directly tied to the positive attention they receive from their community. Status, admiration, prestige—these are the Crowd-Pleaser's crown jewels. When these are threatened, the Crowd-Pleaser's anxiety comes out in full force, and they can think of little else.

Crowd-Pleaser anxiety is triggered by:

- Losing social standing (or the threat of it): This can come from scandal, like Carly's cheating accusation, or from loss of beauty, money, status symbols, position, etc.
- Feeling left behind:They are strongly identified with a sense of belonging and keeping up with their perceived status. In order for Carly to "keep up," she needed to attend an Ivy League school.
- Feeling Lonely: The prospect of being left out or missing out (FOMO!) ignites the Crowd-Pleaser's anxiety. Alice and Carly went to great lengths to maintain their position "in their crowd."
- Being left out: especially of something they were expecting to be included in or invited to, can easily send Crowd-Pleasers into a tailspin.

Crowd-Pleasers deal with their anxiety by:

- Working harder and doubling down on their initial efforts to achieve beauty, status, prestige, or whatever quality is valued by their in-group.
- Making sure they are up-to-date on all the current trends, fashions, gossip, and other topics of conversation: This can include watching all the current hot shows, reading insider publications, going to insider events, etc.
- Practicing skills that will allow them to show off to their in-group: If the Crowd-Pleaser's in-group plays tennis or basketball, for example, they might spend extra time practicing on their own, or hire a trainer to help improve their skills.

Crowd-Pleaser children are a natural extension of their parents' social identity. Therefore, all of the above relates not only to the Crowd-Pleaser's own life, but to their child's life as well. If their child loses social standing, is left behind, or left out, that triggers the Crowd-Pleaser's anxiety in the same way. Similarly, they will deal with this anxiety by pushing their children to work harder, to make sure they are up-to-date and competitive in the relevant skills needed to keep up with their peers.

THE ANXIETY SPIRAL

While any parent would be upset and anxious if their child were accused of cheating, Alice's anxieties centered around the public-image aspect of this crisis: What if others find out? What will they think? Will others think that Carly's a cheater? Will this tarnish our family's reputation? Even if Carly proves her innocence, will others think that she is unworthy of her accomplishments? Will she be ostracized by her friends? What if Carly's friends get into their colleges of choice but Carly doesn't because of this humiliating mark on her record? Will she be forced to go to an unimpressive school which will make her seem mediocre compared to her peers? Will this damage her prospects? How will they be able to show their faces again?

Carly was just as upset as Alice, only she was the primary subject in this potential scandal, and had the most to lose. She was scared and anxious and sought her mother's comfort. Unfortunately, Alice was so overcome with anxiety that she was unable to "sit" with Carly as she cried. Carly needed her mother to be with her, but because Alice's anxiety was so all-consuming, she could not bear to "just be" with her daughter's emotions.

Instead, she went on the attack. Alice blamed the testing company, and even considered suing them for false accusation. She assured Carly that she would clean up the mess and protect her from any further trouble. Alice contacted an attorney to commence an appeal process.

Carly was left with her own anxiety and distress, as well as feelings of guilt for her mother's distress. She began her own therapy to manage the stress of the situation.

Common Crowd-Pleaser pitfalls:

- Disregard Individual Needs: They do not trust their internal barometer and rely heavily on the behaviors and observations of others to gauge progress and success.
- What others think seems to be the primary motivator for most things that Alice does. She spent so much time emphasizing the importance of winning at all costs to her daughters that Carly may have cheated to get a high score on her ACT.
- Lose Their Sense of Self: Because they allow others to define their path, they may lose their individuality. Alice and Carly were so swept up in the hypercompetitive chase that they neglected to consider if an Ivy League school was an ideal match for Carly.
- Susceptible to Peer Pressure: With a tendency to absorb the crowd's anxiety, Crowd-Pleasers are prone to suffer from contagion phenomenon (the ability to directly or indirectly influence the behaviors and emotions of others).Alice and Carly kept track of the test scores all of Carly's friends were achieving. That created a very specific pressure of "Achieve this level of test score or you'll have fallen behind."
- Prone to insular views: Alice became swept up in the cutthroat culture of her specific community; everyone around her wanted their kids to attend an Ivy League school, so it seemed there was

no other option for Carly. (In actuality, there are many excellent schools that suit a wide range of students and their interests.)

FACING THE ANXIETY

As Alice watched Carly suffer, her own anxiety intensified, to the point where she was unable to support her daughter. In order to overcome this and fulfill her role as an emotionally available and supportive parent, Alice needed to learn to manage her own anxiety.

The necessary first step, becoming aware of her anxiety, was easy. Alice's anxiety was unmistakable; she was unable to sleep or eat, and was chronically preoccupied.

Next, we set out to validate Alice's anxiety and disentangle her sense of self-worth from the current situation. This was an understandably anxiety-producing situation and would likely bring up feelings for any parent. It was not wrong for Alice to be distressed or for her to value her public image and social status. Through this process she realized how she had become so caught up in her anxieties that she had lost sight of Carly's individual development, emotionally and characterologically. She was able to see how her anxiety had been influencing her thoughts.

Crowd Pleaser Thought Distortions: Alice, like most Crowd-Pleasers, had been falling into some of the following problematic thought patterns:

- **Black-and-white thinking:** If Carly doesn't get into an Ivy League school, that mean's she's a failure.
- **Catastrophizing:** Carly's future is ruined. She will never amount to anything. She will become a social pariah, or be canceled. Maybe she shouldn't go to school at all until this is resolved.
- **Overgeneralizing:** Of course this would happen to *my* daughter. We have to try so much harder than everyone else to prove our worth. Nothing comes easily to us like it does for the people around us.
- **Labeling:** My daughter is a cheater; I am a bad mother.
- **Blaming:** This is my fault. I should have had her take the test at a site where she didn't know anyone.

By identifying these thoughts as they came up, Alice was able to see the situation more clearly and be less reactive to her anxieties.

Alice went on to clarify her values (family first, being a good mom, raising a healthy daughter), which allowed her to challenge and reframe these thoughts with the following perspectives:

- This experience was an opportunity for self-growth, both for her and her daughter, in the following ways:
- This experience is forcing all of us to take a pause and evaluate what's most important and what we value most (crises have a way of offering this insight).
- Alice and Carly have felt like they've been on "opposing sides" for years. This crisis could be an opportunity for Alice to demonstrate empathy and support for her daughter and remind her that they're on the same team.
- Carly has many positive attributes that she's strengthened over the years: tenacity, determination, grit, and self-advocacy. This experience will not only strengthen those attributes, but also be a chance for her to learn about anxiety and establish ways to manage it. When she gets through this, it will be a reference point for her in future stressful situations: Knowing she was able to get through a devastating experience and emerge stronger, she will be able to do it again.

Alice realized that she had been letting her fears about keeping up appearances cloud her real values: being a supportive and attuned mom and raising emotionally healthy daughters. She set herself on a new path, one that involved seeing her daughter as an individual and partnering with her to find a way forward that worked for her.

FORGING CARLY'S PATH

After much consideration and deliberation, they decided to appeal the testing company's ruling about Carly's test scores. Ultimately, the accusation was lifted. Despite her now spotless academic record and impressive test scores, Carly was deferred (and ultimately not accepted) by her early decision school. However, this did not sting as much as it once would have. Together Alice and Carly had pushed beyond the black-and-white thinking of "Ivy League or Bust." They reexamined their approach to the whole school process, learning to appreciate different schools in a more nuanced way.

During this time of reflection and reconsideration, Carly cast her net wider and considered schools that she had previously thought were "beneath her." She came to appreciate different kinds of schools for their unique values.

Later on, Carly and Alice would refer to this experience as a "blessing in disguise." It forced them to step off of the cultural treadmill, reevaluate, and ultimately reclaim their values. Values, rather than anxieties, became their guiding light.

Carly ended up attending a non–Ivy League school that offered a greater emphasis on business, which was her main interest. The program in question allowed for more internship opportunities and work experience. Alice also went on to approach her younger daughter's college process differently, keeping her values in the driver's seat and her Crowd-Pleaser tendencies in check.

Chapter 7

Chris the Avoider

Chris is the married father of a preteen son and daughter and lives in a New York City suburb known for its liberalism and multiculturalism. For over a decade, he's been a high school English teacher at a progressive private school. He has also published several books and writes short stories that are often published on various writing platforms. Somewhat of a Renaissance man, he has many interests and hobbies which he deeply enjoys, and "relies on to maintain his sanity," from playing music to woodworking and reading.

Highly observant, he considers, questions, and challenges many social norms and cultural tendencies. He is acutely attuned to peers who are prone to being "lemmings," which he intentionally avoids. Though pleasant in his presentation, Chris's cynicism and counterculture mind-set indicate an underlying resentment, dissatisfaction, and frustration with his surroundings. This faintly detectable quality periodically surfaces and manifests in depressive episodes which he's experienced since college. During such times, he's sought therapy, to which he's effectively responded. This depression has resurfaced during intense times of transition or change.

We met shortly after the birth of his first child, his son, Jeremy. I remember him sitting on the couch in my office during our first meeting, wearing a flannel shirt, loosely fitted jeans, sneakers, and a small silver stud in each of his ears. It was clear from his style and demeanor that he had no wish to adhere to the standard social conventions of the fast-paced, hypercompetitive, upper-middle-class New York parenting world.

As a new parent Chris was bothered by the high-strung parents around him and the pressure to follow the commonly accepted parenting "script." Unsurprisingly, given his history, Chris's adjustment to parenthood catalyzed a depressive episode which manifested as a noticeable withdrawal from other people, excessive sleeping, and a heightened irritability.

Throughout the course of our initial sessions, Chris become more comfortable with the idea that being a new parent didn't mean he suddenly needed to adhere to the predominant parenting culture he found himself in. He was still able to parent and live his life according to his values. No stranger to therapy, Chris kept in touch, scheduling sessions with me as needed. I was, therefore, one of the first people he reached out to more than a decade later, to discuss a new dilemma arising around his now preteen son, Jeremy.

WHO ARE AVOIDERS?

Avoiders and Crowd-Pleasers are two sides of the same coin. But while Crowd-Pleasers respond to the conventions and expectations set by their peers by trying to meet or exceed them, Avoiders have the opposite reaction. Avoiders see the pressures and problems Crowd-Pleasers subject themselves to and decide to do the exact opposite. In our current achievement-dominated society, this looks like the seeming rejection of achievement culture altogether.

The more aggressive (pushy, overbearing, overwhelming) people around them are, the more passive and resistant Avoiders become. While this prevents them from being swept up into societal spirals, it can also thwart their pursuit of the things they *do* want. The "aggressive" energies of Avoiders are directed so much toward *resisting* the culture around them that they have little left in their reserves to direct toward their own ambitions and passionate pursuits.

As parents, Avoiders may appear passive, laissez-faire, and noncompetitive on the outside, while behind closed doors, they quietly disapprove of those who accelerate, push, or direct their teens' development. Avoiders believe instead that their teens' development will unfold organically.

Avoider Perks:

- Non-conforming: Unlike the Crowd-Pleaser, Avoiders are not prone to peer pressure. They do not give into the demands of the hyper-achievement culture. They take pride in their uniqueness.
- Maintain perspective: Often concerned with the larger picture, Avoiders don't obsess about the details presented by daily achievement related decisions.
- Confidence in Evolution: Avoiders trust the process and expect that things will organically work out the way that they're supposed to. If things are going to work out anyway, why work so hard at it?

Avoiders are fatalistic—"Everything will work out in the end"—and resistant to engaging in many decisions that burden other parents. They won't spend hours and hours researching the best activities to sign their kids up for; whatever is offered by the school is fine. They won't worry about whether their kid will get into the gifted and talented program; they trust their kids' teachers to let them know if their child should be advanced.

In many ways, the Avoiders' parenting decisions are characterized by their being on the path of least resistance.

CHRIS'S STORY

As with all PARTs, Chris's history sheds light on the origins of his avoidant style. His mother was a vivacious woman, talkative, opinionated, and, at times, overbearing. A stay-at-home mom, she set the tone, cadence, and emotional climate of the household.

The youngest of three children (by a significant margin), Chris's older siblings were loud, boisterous, and competitive. As a young boy, he experienced this busy, bustling home as overwhelming, and he avoided the chaos by withdrawing. He sought solace in his room, spending hours reading and listening to music. Though he was relatively content being alone, there was an innate loneliness that accompanied this tendency. Withdrawing became his way of managing any uncomfortable feelings which arose when dealing with his family. In the presence of any discomfort or conflict he would quietly bow out and not participate. His withdrawal and avoidance of participation was adaptive and protective.

Chris strongly identified with his father, resembling him in appearance and temperament. His father was a quiet man, prone to passivity, deferring to his wife to run the show at home. Many nights after his workday as a corporate executive, his father would retreat to the darkroom he had built in the basement, developing photographs, or he'd spend time in his study, reading professional journals and business-related materials.

Despite his more introverted nature, as a child, Chris yearned to be in the mix, to have a more defined place among his siblings, but he couldn't quite figure out a way to do so. His siblings occupied a lot of physical and emotional space in the family. Chris was unable to fit himself into this dynamic. Because his older siblings' busy schedules required many hours of his mother's time, carpooling and shuttling them to various activities, Chris entertained himself by reading. He read in the car, in ballet school waiting rooms, and on gymnasium and field bleachers. As his mother socialized and gossiped with other mothers, Chris buried himself in science-fiction books.

And when he was not immersed in a book, he quietly and intensely observed the dynamics of other families. Perceptive, thoughtful, and sensitive, Chris often wondered about the inner lives and experiences of the adults around him. He wondered if his mother resented the division of labor in the family, if she wished to work outside of the home, if she was satisfied. He imagined his own future and how he intended to approach his adulthood differently.

Rather than participating, engaging, and competing with his siblings, he eventually "forfeited," retreating even more into himself. This became a habituated style that worked for him. As he got older and pursued a degree in philosophy, he immersed himself in books about other religions, and non-capitalist ideologies.

His rebellion—where he spent his aggressive energy—was internal. He rebelled through learning different ideas and conducting himself differently. Ultimately, his depression was another quiet rebellion, an aggression turned inward against himself. Having spent a majority of his life defining himself as an outsider and rejecting the predominant "competitive culture" he found himself in, Chris was shaken by his preteen son's invitation, and desire, to join a highly competitive soccer league. Suddenly, Chris was faced with the prospect of being forced to join, and participate in, the culture he had spent most of his life trying to avoid.

THE AVOIDER'S DILEMMA

Despite the many problems it creates, achievement culture dominates the world we live in. It's even on the rise. As members of society, it's impossible to avoid completely. Even counterculture movements like the "lying flat" movement in China, or the antiwork subreddit (with 1.8 million followers at the time of this writing) are defined by achievement culture. As parents, especially parents of teens, our social circle expands drastically to incorporate our kids' social lives. And the more our social circle expands, the more difficult this phenomenon is to avoid. This is precisely the dilemma Chris found himself in.

By definition, all PARTs' responses to anxiety are reactionary. For Chris, learning to avoid achievement culture was a protective instinct he'd learned as a child. Chris's response to achievement culture wasn't a carefully considered, nuanced strategy. It was a rejection of achievement culture altogether. A classic "throwing the baby out with the bathwater" scenario, Chris may have been avoiding the negative aspects of achievement culture, but he also wasn't reaping any of the benefits. This was a sacrifice he was willing to make on his own behalf, but he was much more conflicted when it came to his son.

THE SPORTING LIFE

Chris's son Jeremy had been a highly athletic and physical child since birth. Like his parents, he was an early reader and breezed through school assignments. His only difficulty was sitting still in the classroom, which Chris and his wife Anna attributed to his high energy level and the possibility of "understimulation" in the classroom. Yet, unlike other parents who may have proactively requested more challenging material or accelerated work to help Jeremy "reach his potential," they assumed that the school would notify them if a change was necessary, or warranted. Jeremy was drawn to kids whose energy levels matched his. He and his friends raced around their close suburban community on their bikes and skateboards.

Jeremy was passionate about sports, participating in any activity requiring a ball. Up until he started middle school, Chris and Anna had been able to avoid weekend commitments to more organized leagues. They preferred to have the freedom and flexibility to spontaneously decide what they wanted to do, and particularly enjoyed hiking and spending weekends at Anna's parents' country house.

Though Jeremy expressed interest in joining weekend sports leagues, Chris and Anna were reluctant to do so. They knew this was a slippery slope. They feared that once they jumped on this organized-sports wagon, it would be difficult—nearly impossible—to jump off. They feared its momentum and trajectory, knowing that each year the teams became more selective, competitive, and time-consuming. Once-a-week practices and one game per weekend quickly accelerated into multiple practices per week, several weekend games, travel, and expenses. Thus, they tried to avoid it entirely.

While Anna and Chris appreciated and were supportive of their son's athleticism, it was not a world with which they had much experience or familiarity. From their outside perspective and their experience with teens through their work in education, they observed this rapidly intensifying sports spiral: practices ending at nine p.m., students missing class to attend extended tournaments, parents' requests for deadline extensions and excusals, parents working overtime to pay for the expensive leagues and equipment. It didn't seem like a world in which either of them wanted to participate.

Eventually, many years after most of Jeremy's friends had become involved, they reluctantly agreed to Jeremy's participation in the town soccer league. Unexpectedly, and despite the dreaded weekend commitment and feared implication of becoming "soccer parents," they enjoyed this Saturday-morning ritual. They were able to socialize with neighbors, meet more families in the community, and their younger daughter, Olivia, got to play with other neighborhood siblings. It was a surprisingly enjoyable family experience.

Even more surprising was the pleasure they felt watching Jeremy play. He was a standout player, with an agility and skill that outshined many of his peers. While they had consistently prided themselves on their noncompetitive natures, they took great pleasure in his excellence and the joy he exuded while playing. As Jeremy got older, he enjoyed his evolving reputation as an excellent athlete, particularly in soccer. His athleticism was becoming an integral part of his evolving identity.

However, as the years went by, many of their initial fears were realized. The competitiveness and seriousness of the league grew, transforming the ethos surrounding the game. By twelve years old, there were no longer leagues where kids could simply "play for fun." Kids were expected to narrow their focus and commit to one sport per season, to enroll in more serious travel leagues which required more skill and commitment, practices three times per week, and travel games on the weekends. These were the very leagues that Chris and Anna had wanted to avoid, emotionally, financially, and logistically.

Jeremy begged to participate in the competitive travel league that the coaches had recommended for him. Yet, for Chris and Anna, their perceptions of the league, the social lessons it taught, and the implications of that on their son's growth made them anxious. It flew in the face of many of their deep-seated beliefs and values. Until now, they had been able to avoid getting swept up in this high-pressure, hypercompetitive culture.

Already resentful of what he perceived as his parents' disinterest and lack of understanding, conflict arose between Jeremy and his parents. Unable to decide, Anna and Chris delayed enrolling him, pushed off any discussions, and avoided addressing it with him (with an unconscious fantasy that the issue would simply disappear).

This dilemma is not uncommon for many parents, but it presented deeper conflicts for Chris. As a philosophy major in college, he felt entangled in a web of philosophical and existential dilemmas. Internally conflicted and loathe to be hypocritical, he was buried beneath the complexity of the issue. He was paralyzed.

Chris resented the system that was "forcing" his son (and he and his wife) into making this decision. He strongly objected to what he perceived as the culture of the competitive league—the requisite frequency and intensity, the exaggerated self-importance exuded by the coach, its expense, and how it would detract from other activities, including unstructured time. Yet he feared making a decision that would potentially isolate his son from his peers, both socially and athletically. As the other players improved through avid skills training and professionally supervised practices, his son would be "left behind." On every level, this presented a dilemma for him.

UNDERSTANDING THE AVOIDER'S ANXIETY

Avoiders like to keep things simple, straightforward, and within their realm of understanding. Like a procrastinator who unconsciously anticipates feeling frustrated and incompetent by specific tasks, the Avoider delays or avoids making decisions where they're at risk of being overwhelmed by opinions or choices. They are prone to denying or minimizing the long-term significance of decisions. Unlike helicopter parents who manage their anxiety by acting, Avoiders control their anxiety through bypassing action entirely. They are not particularly reliant on a sense of agency and often relinquish decisions to chance. Avoiders may also be closet perfectionists who disengage from participation because they cannot tolerate feelings of imperfection or perceived failure: "If I'm not going to do it perfectly, then I will not even try."

Avoider anxiety triggers:

- Feeling forced or pressured to act: The more pressure they feel, the more avoidant they become.
- Aggression, conflict, or the prospect of conflict: Naturally conflict-averse, Avoiders withdraw or detach from situations rather than engaging in conflict.
- Fear of Emotional Flooding: Even the prospect of possibly becoming overwhelmed is often enough to trigger Avoider anxiety.
- Obsessing and overthinking (or the perceived need to do either): Faced with the need to wade through and evaluate multiple choices and opinions, Avoiders would rather opt out entirely.

Avoiders deal with their anxiety by:

- Withdrawing from and/or avoiding anxiety-producing situations
- Resisting pressure to act
- Shutting down/becoming paralyzed/freezing

As parents, Avoiders are very passive, allowing their children to make their own decisions and engaging in the path of least resistance when faced with school or extracurricular decisions. They trust that things will work out, and may view peers as exaggerating when they speak about the importance of making school or extracurricular decisions for their kids.

THE ANXIETY SPIRAL

While this dilemma had been brewing for several months, Chris had not made mention of it until the pressure to make the decision was near. He had consciously avoided discussing it in his therapy, as it was so anxiety-producing and fraught.

As he threw himself on the couch, slouching and leaning his head back in disbelief, he began, "This has been going on for months, but I couldn't bear to face it."

"Yes, many of us fear that talking about something will make it feel more real," I said, "bringing up stuff that we'd like to protect ourselves from feeling." I was trying to highlight the protective motives behind his avoidance, rather than shaming him.

"This is the stuff about being a dad that I can't stand. It's such bull****," he said, with palpable irritation.

"It often feels easier in the short term to avoid it—to not deal with it, and hope that the dilemma goes away or sorts itself out," I reflected.

"Yup, that would've been nice!" he said resigned and sarcastically.

This had been a well-developed pattern for Chris: passivity and avoidance, hoping that the issue would just go away. I knew that part of what he was avoiding was having to sift through and manage many layers of complex and uncomfortable feelings.

"We all avoid things when we anticipate feeling overwhelming or painful emotions," I said.

"Yup," he said. "I know those feelings well."

"Ahhh, the relief of putting off dealing with things. I don't want to be competitive, but I can avoid and procrastinate with the best of them!" I joked, having already confessed my own long history of avoidance.

From my previous experience with him and my intimate familiarity with avoidance, I attempted to address some of the underlying catalyzers of his avoidant tendency. I reminded him that his avoidance was his attempt to protect himself from overwhelm and from being controlled (by overbearing "authorities").

As our sessions continued, I offered reference points in his history where he had challenged his avoidant impulse, reminding him of other times when he was able to sift through a complicated web of anxieties that had accumulated, ultimately leading to a resolution that aligned with his values. I assured him that we'd do the same again, slowly, piece by piece. And that when he became overwhelmed, we would take breaks—no forcing him. I reassured him that he could tolerate the discomfort, that he would have support (we'd do it together), and that he'd come to a solution that he could live with. And perhaps, most importantly, that he would set the pace; I wouldn't control, force, push, or impose (which would only catalyze his avoidance).

From his many years of therapy, Chris knew his avoidance pattern well. The more aggressive (pushy, overbearing, overwhelming) people around him were, the more passive and resistant he became. While this prevented his being swept up into societal spirals, it also thwarted his pursuit of the things he *did* want. His own "aggressive" energies were directed so much toward resisting that he had little left in his reserves to direct toward his own ambitions and passionate pursuits.

Through treatment, Chris had learned that his depression was the outgrowth of many factors—his genetics, family dynamics, learned patterns of avoiding aggression, and his tendency to turn his aggressive feelings inward, toward himself. This fueled his avoidance, and the more avoidant he became, the more his depression worsened.

Common Avoider pitfalls:

- The Avoider misses out on significant decisions. Their passivity can engender feelings of misunderstanding in their children. The avoidance denies the child and the parent the essential feelings of efficacy and mastery—the ability to learn from mistakes and endure failures.
- Avoiders may be prone to under-responsiveness, muting their innate emotional response and making them unable to adequately mirror emotions.
- Avoiders may be prone to procrastination.

- Avoiders thwart their healthy competitive and aggressive urges, leading to underperforming, underachievement, and dissatisfaction.
- By not throwing their hat in the ring, Avoiders miss out on or deny themselves potential moments of joy, competence, or mastery.
- Avoiders become myopic in their resistance such that they overlook significant details and nuances of the situation, minimizing the positives and magnifying the negatives.
- Quick to reject commonly held norms, Avoiders are unable to creatively problem-solve to find solutions that more closely resemble their beliefs.

FACING THE ANXIETY

As we disentangled Chris's history from his current dilemma, he was able see the situation more clearly. He became aware of his anxiety and he challenged his thinking, particularly about the significance that his son's athletic desires/inclinations represented to him. More specifically, he realized:

- He was anxious about "the implications" of being the father of an athlete, and he was anxious about who his son might become.
- He feared that Jeremy would be surrounded by toxic masculinity and become what he perceived/judged as a "stereotypical jock," possessing/representing attributes that Chris avoided and loathed (anxious thought patterns, e.g., preexisting beliefs and forecasting).
- He was anxious that his schedule, values, and influence over his son would be overshadowed or even consumed by the league—what he had witnessed growing up in his own family.
- These fears paralyzed him and prevented him from dealing with the issue at hand.

FINDING A NEW WAY

Rather than avoiding addressing the issue with his son, Chris realized that he needed to be more active in expressing himself; he couldn't punt to his wife or forfeit. He realized that his values would not be overshadowed and that he could assert them more clearly. (He had to overcome his fear that his life would be overtaken, the way it had in childhood.) He had to direct his aggression outward, rather than retreating, channeling it in useful and values-aligned ways.

As he disentangled his anxiety, he was able to clarify what he *did* want for his son: to gain experience in a league that did not usurp the family's weekends or bank accounts or values. With this clarification, Chris actively researched leagues to find one where the coaching style and mission aligned with his—where fun, moderation, and challenge were integrated.

FOLLOWING HIS NORTH STAR

Rather than enrolling Jeremy in the league that many of his current friends were pursuing, he found a slightly less geographically convenient league which practiced what they preached. This program's design aligned with Chris's family and personal values:

- They adhered to a strict one-day-a-week practice and one-game-per-weekend schedule.
- They offered *optional* practice an additional day of the week.
- Coaches had been trained in a particular method/philosophy that prohibited shaming players as well as parents' sideline coaching.
- They offered an optional busing service to transport coaches and players to travel games, with the express purpose of reducing parental inconvenience.
- Games concluded by noon so that players were able to socialize, spend time with family, and engage in other activities.
- Weekday practices concluded by six p.m. to enable players to have time to attend to their studies, eat dinner with their families, and get important rest.

This led to many discussions with Jeremy about how to effectively make values-aligned decisions, identifying what was most important to him, particularly regarding the implications for the rest of the family and Jeremy's interests and competencies. Perhaps most importantly, this revised approach proved satisfying for both Jeremy and his parents.

Chapter 8

Bruce the Clairvoyant

Julie and Bruce were at a stalemate with their daughter, Madeline—a seemingly unresolvable, uncompromisable conflict that they had never encountered together before. In her thirteen years, Madeline had been compliant, self-directed, highly motivated, and mature—a classic first-born. Yet, in the spring of 2020, with an international pandemic roaring, she abruptly declared her decision to quit ballet.

Until this point, Madeline had been a serious and talented dancer, spending four days a week as well as many weekends in the studio for classes, rehearsals, and individualized instruction. Like his wife who had enjoyed contemporary dance throughout college, Bruce was convinced that his daughter was a born dancer. Characterologically, she was devoted, disciplined, and precise, and physically, she was graceful, lithe, and flexible.

Following her early participation in the neighborhood dance school, Bruce eagerly transferred her to a more rigorous and professional school, one which he believed would cultivate her innate skills and advance her to a professional level. As he had predicted, Madeline steadily rose to the high-level classes, becoming a standout student in the program.

As Madeline became more involved in the ballet school's culture, she was invited to participate in its highly regarded dance troupe, and she was awarded lead roles in its performances. This confirmed Bruce's beliefs about his daughter's abilities and perpetuated his hopes and expectations of her continued progress. In fact, until the unexpected pandemic hiatus, neither she nor her parents or teachers had ever considered the possibility of her discontinuing—until this abrupt halt.

Naturally, Julie and Bruce were bemused by her uncharacteristic sudden change of heart. Through multiple conversations with Madeline, they tried to make sense of this seemingly impulsive decision, attributing it to the awkwardness of virtual dance classes or the immediate relief she'd experienced, having a break from the busy schedule. Julie and Bruce pleaded with her to reconsider, or at least to postpone her decision until she had resumed in-person classes. But Madeline had made up her mind; she was adamant about stopping.

This created an understandable dilemma for Julie and Bruce. They were loath to allow her to forgo the many opportunities associated with her dance career, yet they felt powerless to change her mind.

While both parents were understandably concerned, Bruce was especially unable to accept Madeline's withdrawal from the program. Known for his persistence and persuasiveness, he refused to let it go. Using his full range of tactics—from kindness to firmness, from bribes to punishments, from demands to compromise—his every interaction with his daughter either conveyed his explicit disapproval about her decision or a subtext of disappointment and resentment. Eventually, Madeline grew tired of his shaming, so she shut him out completely, refusing to speak or engage with him at all.

The mounting tension and conflict between Madeline and Bruce erupted into an epic screaming match—a battle which Madeline stopped dead in its tracks, literally, when she threatened suicide. Obviously concerned, her parents encouraged her to see a therapist, and she agreed.

WHO ARE CLAIRVOYANTS?

Clairvoyants' special skill is their ability to detect and nurture gifts and abilities in others, particularly their children. They are observant and attuned to what lies beneath the surface—qualities that may or may not be apparent or appreciated by others, but that if appropriately tended can reach extraordinary levels of success in the future. They find pleasure in envisioning what could happen if this skill is developed and eventually flourishes, and they find comfort in believing that their predictions will be fulfilled.

Like the visual distortions created by a crystal ball, the Clairvoyant's psychological lens can magnify the importance of their child's current attributes. Often, such distortions propel their fantasies; they are almost convinced of ways that the quality will flourish and benefit the child in the future. They highlight what seems less obvious to others, or move what might be in the background of another's visual field to the fore.

Clairvoyants also envision that this identified attribute is so central and meaningful to the future that it warrants more focus and attention, magnifying its current importance. They can foresee the gratification that their child—and they—will feel when their prediction is realized: "I saw it in him when he was small, and I focused on it throughout his upbringing. As a result, he has succeeded."

Once the Clairvoyant has developed their vision, they devise a plan to work toward its realization. They think that everyone has their own "thing" that separates them from others, and that this "thing" needs to be identified at an early age so that it may be honed and cultivated well before adulthood.

Clairvoyant Perks:

- Observant: Clairvoyants watch their teens closely—seeing into their potential and envisioning its future benefit.
- Maximize Skills: Once Clairvoyants identify their child's strengths, they go to great lengths to hone them.

MEET MADELINE

Upon first meeting with Madeline over a teleconference line—since the pandemic had shut down in-person appointments—I was struck by her presentation, which reminded me of the TV character Doogie Howser, a child prodigy who practices medicine as a teenager. From the distorted computer screen angle, her exaggeratedly prominent glasses dominated her delicate thirteen-year-old facial features, a metaphor for her pseudo-adultness.

In a highly cerebral, bookish manner, she described the recent conflict with her father. And while she readily and explicitly denied any desire to die, she was overwrought with frustration and sadness. She deeply resented her father's bullishness and what she perceived to be his blatant disregard of her wishes. In the heat of the argument, feeling trapped and without any options, death seemed like her only escape. Together we concluded that her suicidal threat was a desperate plea to be heard and understood, which we agreed to do in therapy.

Madeline's assurances that she did not have intentions or a plan to act on her suicidal ideation allowed us to create a plan to address the conflict. Together, we set the stage for our work in therapy. I made clear to her that I did not have an agenda or an investment in her reversing her decision. I was more interested in hearing her, to listen and understand her—not the "her" that others wanted her to be, but her-*self*. From there, we would figure out ways to translate our understanding to her parents. Madeline expressed relief and eagerness to begin the process.

Through our weekly meetings, Madeline reflected on her feelings toward dance from the previous months, before and during the first six months of the pandemic. In doing so, she realized that not only did she *not* miss ballet, but she was thrilled to be away from it. Insightfully, she explained her gradually changing relationship with dance.

During her elementary and middle school years, ballet had been the source of much-needed structure and routine, aligning with her perfectionist tendencies. She speculated that her dance teachers' favoritism and admiration appealed to her younger, more compliant, and quiet self. Yet, as she approached adolescence, her needs and preferences had been shifting. She had started to grow weary of the rigidity and the stifling pressure of the ballet world, and she yearned for more time to connect with her peers in other environments. Madeline speculated that her parents' and teachers' expectations and enthusiasm, coupled with her people-pleasing and compliant nature, had been propelling her dance momentum for longer than she had realized.

The unexpected downtime of the pandemic made space for her to reflect, reconsider, and evaluate. For the first time, and as an emerging adolescent, she was considering ideas and interests that were separate from those of her parents and those she had pursued during her childhood. She was yearning to direct and express herself differently than she had done in the past.

In therapy sessions, Madeline relished the lack of agenda and the freedom to discuss whatever she wanted. She excitedly introduced many emerging areas of interest—friends, politics, current events, and social dynamics. It was noteworthy that she rarely, if ever, spoke about dance. Her heart and soul had shifted their focus, and ballet was no longer center stage.

Inspired by the upcoming presidential election, she found herself spending much of her unstructured time immersed in politics. She seemed to have an insatiable curiosity and acquired extensive knowledge about the country's history and leadership. Through sharing her evolving perspectives and beliefs in sessions, we drew connections between her interpretations of the political landscape, her emotions, and her family dynamics.

Madeline was acutely attuned to political leadership style and how some political leaders overpowered, suppressed, and marginalized the voices of many citizens. She identified organizations that shared her deep concerns about the country's future, and supported and promoted their views through social media. With a forum to express and explore ideas, we drew some insights and parallels into her own psychology, themes which mirrored her conflicts with her father: the importance of having a voice, self-empowerment, accessing support, and finding effective ways to convey opposing beliefs.

MADELINE'S PARENTS

During this initial crisis, I had several meetings with Madeline's parents to provide them with my preliminary assessment and treatment plan. As our work together progressed, and I gained a richer understanding of Madeline and the family dynamics, I periodically met with her parents to facilitate parent–teen communication and to offer additional guidance as needed. And given her father's heavy-handedness and the intensity of the conflict between father and daughter, I met with him individually for several sessions, as well.

BRUCE'S VISION

Bruce presented as a confident, outspoken man with a large personality and sense of conviction. He seemed especially well suited for his executive position in the music industry where he rubbed elbows with famous musical artists and regularly negotiated seven-figure music deals. Well

known in his field for his keen predictions of music trends, he identified and worked with many cutting-edge and up-and-coming musicians.

Understandably, he used this keen sense with his own children,
particularly Madeline. He knew the value of having a passion and the
importance of parental support. Many of the professional musicians
he knew attributed their success to their parents' ardent support and
dedication.

Raised in the Midwest, Bruce's parents worked overtime to maintain
what he describes as a very middle-class, blue-collar lifestyle. The
middle son of his parents' three children, Bruce was often cast in his
older brother's shadow, particularly when it came to sports. While they
were both athletic, his brother was an extraordinary baseball player
with unmatched innate ability. Although Bruce admired and envied his
brother's gifts, he believed that his brother lacked passion, discipline,
and drive—that he didn't appreciate his abilities and took them for
granted. In fact, by the time his brother had reached his senior year of
high school, he had missed so many practices and demonstrated such
little commitment to the team that his coaches summarily removed him
from the roster. "A waste of talent!" Bruce lamented.

Conscious of his brother's reputation, he explained further.

"I found my own sport—wrestling. This was *my thing*. I loved it,
made great friends on the team, and spent a lot of time practicing and
trying to improve. And I did. It's so important to have a thing that
you're good at, that you identify with, and that makes you special. I
loved being known as Bruce the wrestler. It's important to find your
children's strengths and foster them so that they have their thing.

"Yes," he said emphatically. "I want each of my kids to have something in addition to school—something that sets them apart and that
rounds them out as people. And Madeline's is ballet! She's got the raw
talent! She's the only toddler I know who looked graceful even when
she was learning to walk.

"And when you see talent, you want to make something of it," I
reflected. "Few parents would allow their extraordinarily talented child
to forgo opportunities for excellence! This would be a dilemma any caring parent, and it has particular significance to you, given your history.
Wasted talent and forgone opportunities remind you of your brother."

He humorously retorted, "Great—send my suicidal daughter to
therapy and I get psychoanalyzed. Is this what we signed up for?"

THE ANXIETY SPIRAL

Bruce was determined to harness and channel Madeline's dance abilities toward further advancement in the company. He wanted to ensure that she reaped the full benefits of this rare gift—that she didn't miss out on opportunities to progress and maximize her strength. The prospect of his daughter's quitting dance catalyzed his anxiety. He feared that she failed to see what he was able to envision. Thus, he intensified the pressure and became more insistent on her continuing. This pressure alienated his daughter and made her feel *not* seen and heard—the opposite of what he intended.

As I invited him to talk about this dynamic, his Clairvoyant floodgates opened, his anxiety, his anxious thoughts, and his anxious parenting behaviors coming into full view.

Bruce began, "This kid has no idea how good she has it. How lucky she is to be so smart *and* a standout dancer in a known dance company. This will help her in the future! Even if she decides not to become a dancer, what college wouldn't want a student with this level of accomplishment in addition to her grades! Students in the top colleges have something else that they excel in other than school. And she has it in the palm of her hand!"

"You see all of the benefits of her excelling in dance," I reflected. "It pains you to think that she'd let that go."

Revealing his many corresponding anxious thoughts, he continued.

"I think this decision of hers is based on laziness. Ballet was getting harder and more demanding, and she didn't want to put in the work. She only dedicates herself to things that come easily to her. Is she going to quit every time something gets more difficult? And even if she thinks she's 'taking a break' now, she can't just pick up where she left off. The school is not going to allow her to come in and out as she pleases. She quits now, this is the end of dance for her. I cannot let that happen!"

"The idea of her quitting is so distressing, and you have many thoughts about what would happen if she were to quit," I said. "It sounds like the way you've described your brother, and I imagine you want to prevent her from going down his unambitious path," I said.

"Being kicked off the baseball team was just the beginning for my brother," Bruce said. "After that, he became a perennial quitter. He left college after three semesters; he's quit every job he ever had. He even quits every relationship before it gets too serious. He's never done much with his life. And he could have done so much more!"

"So, the prospect of not knowing your gifts, or not using them to the best of your ability and quitting—those things have a particular sting for you?" I said.

"If I had had my brother's talent, I know exactly what would have happened. I would have worked myself to the bone, made every contact possible, and made it to the minor leagues. I know that he could have, but he preferred quitting."

As he shook his head emphatically, he paused and thought for a moment.

"I will not let my daughter waste this gift! Quitting and wasting her talent that we saw and cultivated over all these years is not an option. She's headed for great things, I know!"

"Yes, you're anxious about her stopping," I agreed. We discussed his anxieties, his strong wish to protect his daughter, and how his worries were preventing him from seeing the rest of his daughter more clearly.

"It's not about anxiety," Bruce said. "It's about logic. Stop now, lose out. That's a fact."

MADELINE'S MANY GIFTS

All the while, Madeline was becoming more involved in the school's debate team and was testing the waters of writing articles and opinion pieces for the school newspaper. In our sessions, her somewhat reserved presentation shifted to joyful, alive, and funny. She was developing new friendships with her peers who shared her interests in history and politics. She admired her debate advisor's activism and developed a strong connection to her as a new role model. Her adolescent self was emerging and blossoming!

FACING FUTURE PROJECTIONS

At a later session with Bruce, we discussed the way he compared Madeline's behavior to his brother's.

"Yes, it was a fact for your brother," I said. "I see the connection you're drawing and how determined you are to prevent Madeline from going down the same path as your brother." Attempting to challenge his anxious thought pattern, I asked, "Are there any differences between Madeline and your brother?"

"Well, of course," Bruce replied. "She has had a completely different upbringing than we did. We're around much more. We have our finger on the pulse of what's going on, and we have the resources to support our kids with their interests."

"The similarities to your brother make you draw these conclusions. It seems that you're overlooking some significant facts in the equation. I'm struck by Madeline's extensive knowledge of politics, the time and investment she's made in her debate team and the school newspaper— the hours of research, the commitment to her team, and the leadership she's already established. Utterly impressive!" I said.

Bruce sat quietly. His anxiety had impaired his psychological vision, blinding him to the gifts that Madeline was so clearly exhibiting. In his efforts to prevent his daughter from following his brother's unsatisfying path, he had myopically focused on her ballet trajectory. Once he had disentangled his brother's history from his daughter's developing self, he began to appreciate her growth, change, and agency.

Bruce began to identify and validate the origins of his cascading worries: Madeline becoming like his brother, fear of her squandering her gifts and not living up to her potential, his fear of her living with regret. He saw that when he focused on what he predicted would certainly happen, he became more indignant, rigid, and myopic in his interactions with Madeline. As he became more aware of how his anxieties influenced his thoughts and actions, he was able to view the situation through a wider and more flexible lens. And from this expanded viewpoint, he could approach the dilemma (and Madeline) with the control and reason he prided himself on.

Bruce wanted what was best for his daughter, and for her to be happy and fulfilled as an independent adult. And what he valued *now* was meeting her where she was developmentally. He acknowledged that as an emerging adolescent, she needed to emotionally separate from her parents and develop an identity, including making some of her own decisions. And he appreciated that if he were to override her need to do so, he would thwart her development. He developed a deeper appreciation for her need to figure out who she was, to acquire more agency over her direction, identify her passions, and develop a sense of competence and mastery. He wanted to support her and her self-expression (even if it differed from how he defined it), for her to engage with her peers, and to identify new role models and mentors in addition to her parents.

In ongoing interactions with Madeline, Bruce conveyed his respect for the necessary shifts in their relationship. After all, and as he said, "I've never raised a teenager before. I can't predict the future of what will happen—and that's a tough pill to swallow!" He approached their previously perceived power struggle as a collaborative decision-making process that would be guided by his clearly articulated values.

Madeline demonstrated the many ways that her current pursuits were, in fact, meeting his parenting values, and that her deepening involvement in the school newspaper and the debate team were better suited for her growing sense of self. She yearned for a place to express her views and ideas, cherished her burgeoning relationships with peers and advisors, and felt a sense of ownership over her decisions.

UNDERSTANDING CLAIRVOYANT ANXIETY

Clairvoyants are observant, attuned, and strategic. They manage the uncertainty of the future by identifying strengths and maximizing them to secure a forecasted future success. Through their careful predictions of the skill's future value, they bind their anxieties by investing in fostering, fertilizing, and developing them. As parents, Clairvoyants are anxious about the prospect of their child squandering or overlooking a gift or skill and forgoing them in childhood. They fear their child will lose out on potential opportunities for advancement, or worse yet, that their child doesn't possess any exceptional qualities. Mediocrity is the Clairvoyant's nemesis.

Clairvoyant anxiety is triggered by:

- Mediocrity:The prospect of their child being mediocre; they fear the thought of their child becoming a jack of all trades but master of none.

- Being Unnoticed:They fear that their child will blend in with the crowd, without any identifiable strengths or exceptionality to build on for their future.
- Missed Opportunities:Clairvoyants fear that they may overlook or fail to maximize any opportunity for their child to develop a skill they envision will hold future benefits or gains for them in adulthood (scholarships, eventual careers, financial security).

Clairvoyant parents deal with their anxiety by:

- Directing and harnessing their child's observable attributes into a productive channel that could lead them to future success (e.g., directing an oppositional and argumentative teen toward a career as a prosecutor; a tall child to basketball or modeling).
- Seeking evidence to support their visions; a child's demonstrated progress confirms the parent's insights and reinforces their pursuits.
- Envisioning the future possibilities of a skill's development and devising a plan to meet the intended goal.
- Becoming angry and controlling.

Common Clairvoyant pitfalls:

- Singularly focused: Their skill of clairvoyance negatively impacts their perspective. They become so myopic and reliant on their future vision that they lose sight of the teen's present emotional status and developmental stage.
- Inflexible:They are so driven and intentional in their plan that they become rigid, inflexible, and binary in their thinking.
- Lose Sight of the Present:They become so narrowly focused that they thwart the emergence of their child's expanding interests, skills, abilities, and desires through this significant developmental period.

COMMON CLAIRVOYANT THOUGHT TRAPS

Through communications with Madeline and several parenting sessions, Bruce became aware of and began to challenge several anxious thought patterns which were fueling the conflict with his daughter.

- **Binary thinking:** As far as Bruce was concerned, it was now or never. If Madeline did not continue ballet, she would lose this central part of her identity and not have *a thing*. In his eyes, she was either a dancer, or she was not. If she stopped dancing now, her future as a dancer was ruined.
- **Catastrophizing:** Bruce was convinced that Madeline would be lost without dance. He saw this as a quality that made her stand out, and believed she would not have anything else to differentiate her college application from that of another top student. He believed that she was jeopardizing her future success by quitting.
- **Magnification:** Bruce became so focused on ballet that he minimized many other significant qualities Madeline demonstrated skill and interest in. He underestimated the value of her political interests, as well as her developmental need to express herself and direct her own course.
- **Deep-seated beliefs:** If you have a gift, you must use it. (And there is only one way to do so!)
- **Labeling:** She is a quitter (like my brother!).

As Bruce became more aware of the impact of his anxiety on his thinking and his behavior toward his daughter, he began to challenge his thoughts. This enabled him to manage his anxiety differently and shift his focus toward what Madeline wanted.

OVERCOMING CLAIRVOYANT ANXIETY

Part of being attuned to our children is recognizing and appreciating our children's individual gifts and strengths, doing what we can to cultivate them so they will flourish. Our children's innate skills can be pleasurable for us to observe and can quell our anxieties about the future. When this anxiety goes unchecked, it can lead us astray. And when that's the case, here's a guide to help you get back on course.

- The first step is realizing that you have anxiety. Your efforts to have some certainty about the future are part of anxiety's workshop.
- The second step is to establish your goal. Since your goal is to help your teen tap into their innate skills, make sure that the current expression of the skill is engendering overall pleasure in your teen—that they are still invested, committed, and interested in the activity. And make sure that your investment in their continuing is not overriding their interest.
- The third step is to recognize that your anxiety is interfering with the process. This enables you to help your teen look within and better understand the shift in interest. By owning your anxiety, you can more clearly refocus on your teen's current emotions and needs.
- The fourth step is to express your intentions to your teen, using specific language and "I statements": "I want you to feel good about what you're doing, engaged in something that makes you feel alive and fulfilled. I want to help you find what that is—for you, not for me."

Realizing that he needed to shift his approach toward his daughter, Bruce articulated his intentions, desires, and anxieties. He moved from a self-protective stance to a self-reflective one. Rather than reacting, he walked Madeline through his thought process, owning his anxieties, articulating his intentions and values. His anxiety had gotten him so far ahead of himself that he was missing what was right in front of him. This opened up lines of communication with his daughter.

As Bruce became more aware of his anxiety, he gained more intellectual agility. He was better equipped to creatively problem-solve and stay in the moment, rather than predicting the future. He honored Madeline's developmental needs to emotionally separate from her parents, develop an identity based on her interests and desires, experience a sense of belonging among like-minded peers, develop her own voice and self-awareness, and take agency over the direction of her life.

Chapter 9

Carol and Jim, the Shepherds

I began working with twenty-four-year-old Max shortly after his moving to New York City following a protracted post-college job search. Though not particularly symptomatic at the time, Max's parents, Carol and Jim, arranged for him to be in therapy for additional support— essentially, to help him "stay on track." With a history of attentional, "language processing issues," anxiety, and what they referred to as "general immaturity," they wanted an extra set of eyes on him. Assuring me that her son had given her permission to share information, Carol agreed that he would contact me to schedule his session.

Several weeks later, Carol contacted me, frustrated that her son had not called to make an appointment. She suggested that she should make it, saying, "He's pretty overwhelmed and is not great at time management. It's probably easier that I schedule it for him." As if thinking out loud she reviewed a litany of caveats. "It will need to be after five. He typically leaves work by five, but then he may want to grab a snack, and it'll take him some time to get to your office. Would you have availability at six p.m. Monday through Thursday? I wouldn't want to schedule him on a Friday in case his team goes out for happy hour. Also, he's still on our health insurance, so you can send the bills to me." And she provided her address.

I requested that Max email his appointment confirmation, which he compliantly sent, cc'ing his parents.

MEET MAX

The following Wednesday evening, Max dutifully arrived at the session. Standing at six-foot-four, with broad shoulders and a notably deep voice, his physical appearance conveyed strength and virility. His auburn hair was neatly parted, and he was dressed in the casual conventional professional attire of his peers. His light blue oxford shirt was neatly tucked into his khakis, held up by a belt which matched his brown laced "work" shoes. He was dressed for his part as adult. He spoke with extreme politeness and deference; it was evident to me that he had been raised in an environment that emphasized good manners and social etiquette.

Respectfully responding to my questions about his purpose for therapy, he reminded me of an actor with a newly memorized script. Beneath his monotone and parroted manner was a detectable unease; he had burdened and "lost boy" qualities about him.

Despite this presentation, Max denied feeling any anxiety or depression. He claimed that since he was in the throes of a big adjustment to a new city, and a new job, he had "agreed" with his parents that the additional support might be helpful. He shared information about his entry-level position in a small marketing firm, and expressed his relief in having a "good job, where I'm learning a lot, and meeting a lot of people."

Like his college peers, he had always expected that he'd move to New York and live the typical post-college life. And with his parents' coordination, he was subletting the second bedroom in his cousin's apartment while her roommate moved in with a boyfriend. He appreciated the financial benefits and the additional family support of this arrangement.

For the next several months Max compliantly attended sessions, claiming to be happy and denying any anxiety or sadness, yet still presenting as somewhat disconnected and flat, with a heaviness about him. And while he seemed somewhat of a shell of a person, I assumed that his authentic self would reveal itself in time. I kept my eye out for any indications of what lay beneath his ultra-polite and seemingly passionless surface.

Periodically, Max's parents left voicemail messages expressing their behind-the-scenes concerns or information that they believed "might be helpful" for me to know in my work with their son. I noted both the content of their messages and the way they offered it.

Parents' participation in the treatment of adolescents, late adolescents, and young adults varies, and is determined on a case-by-case basis. Barring a crisis or extenuating circumstance, it is rare for parents of a young adult to have this degree of contact with me. Thus, Carol and Jim's communications were emblematic of their family's dynamics and boundaries, and their experienced perceptions of their son. From a legal and clinical standpoint, I was unable to share confidential information with them, but I could receive information from them. With their knowledge, I notified him of their calls, and with his permission and authorization, I would periodically contact or respond to them.

WHO ARE SHEPHERDS?

Shepherds have a great historical context in literature and religion. A shepherd takes great care of his flock and may even put his own life in danger to keep them out of harm's way. Similar to the biblical "good shepherd," the Shepherd parent is a watchful protector who uses their life experience to guide their children to necessary and safe destinations; like shepherds throughout history, Shepherd parents would lay down their lives for their sheep. In turn, the sheep remain faithful, trusting, and compliant, and follow their leader. Shepherds are good leaders and know what they're doing. They are familiar with the landscape, rely on their good sense of direction, and have confidence in their abilities to guide.

Like Crowd-Pleasers, Shepherd parents are accustomed to the herd mentality and group conventions. Shepherds are unlikely to differentiate one sheep from the next; they are less focused on individuality, and discourage any straying from the pack. The Shepherd fundamentally believes that their flock is unable to care for itself. With their familiarity and experience with the landscape and confidence in their ability to navigate it, they expect to be followed. "Follow me. I know the way. I can lead you into adulthood."

Shepherd Perks:

- Good Executive Functioning: Shepherds are organized (keep their sheep in orderly fashion), planful, and prepared. They're familiar with the path and have a planned steps toward their destination.
- Focused: Shepherds remain on their identified route and do not go astray. The are rarely distracted from their plan.
- Protective: Shepherds keep close watch on their sheep to ensure that they are well cared for and directed.

THE WORSENING PROBLEM

Later in the year, I received frantic messages and emails from Max's parents. "We're not sure if Max is discussing this with you, but he received a *bad* review at work! Clearly his boss is unhappy with him. We're not sure if Max realizes the potential implications of this, but it sounds like she's laying the groundwork to firing him!"

Yet when I met with Max later that week, he seemed as genuinely unfazed by his evaluation as he did by his parents' interference in his therapy. "I spoke to my boss, and it's fine. I don't always work as quickly as she'd like, but she's okay with that," he said dismissively.

Max offered little insight into the obvious incongruity between his parents' worry and his casual response, shrugging it off as if he had developed immunity to their involvement. I encouraged him to speak to them and offered future family therapy sessions to Carol and Jim, which they readily accepted.

During several family sessions in which his parents phoned in as Max and I met in the office, I was struck by the chasm between their respective perceptions—his parents' concerns about Max's performance and his boyish optimism about its outcome. I appreciated the predicament these loving parents found themselves in, sensing a situation that was likely going off the rails, feeling protective, desperate to prevent him from going further astray. I felt my own anxiety rising, but Max appeared unaffected.

In his parents' attempts to mitigate this situation from devolving further, they employed many of their previously effective shepherding techniques, imploring him to speak to his boss, offering him talking points, and suggesting several communication approaches. They encouraged him to work on the weekends, and even offered to proofread some of his work to preserve his declining job security. Their anxieties were rising, and they were feeling increasingly ineffective when it came to shepherding him through this work experience. They feared the cascading impact of this failure on his confidence and career trajectory.

From their viewpoint, his adulthood was not getting off to a successful start; instead, it was going woefully off course. Their worst fears were coming true: He was truly disabled/deficient, and unable to function independently. They didn't feel this was merely a matter of catastrophizing; they believed their fears were well founded.

THE ORIGINS OF THEIR WORRIES

It seems that Max's early diagnosis of learning difficulties made his parents anxious, and ashamed. They feared that he would be chronically hampered by his challenges, and if they were revealed, he would be treated as intellectually inferior. They perceived his "disabilities" as limitations or cognitive deficiencies for which *they* needed to compensate. They feared that these labels would lower his self-esteem and negatively differentiate him from his peers. In fact, they were so focused on the ways the learning difficulties had differentiated him from traditional schooling that they were unable to appreciate and highlight the many strengths that he likely had.

Unfortunately, their attempts to scaffold him inadvertently erected barriers to his independent growth. He was not developing his own understanding and methods to work with his challenges and to use his strengths. Max's current detachment and passivity seemed to be reflective of his lack of agency or ownership of his challenges. Their well-intended efforts to help him were unwittingly hampering him. In their efforts to protect him from pain, they preemptively felt his emotions for him! He had grown so accustomed to his parents' shepherding that he hadn't developed or exercised muscles of self-direction, emotional regulation/responsiveness, or coping. He had merely strengthened the muscles of either ignoring or blindly following his parents' directions.

Intent on keeping him on course, throughout college Max's parents had kept themselves apprised of his daily schedule, proofread his papers, and made sure that he adhered to deadlines. And during breaks, they secured "internships" at his uncle's law firm where he often helped with manual labor and menial administrative tasks, with which he dutifully complied.

Upon Max's graduation, they tapped every professional and personal connection, made introductions, and networked. Carol and Jim methodically researched and pursued jobs for their son, role-played interviews, reviewed his techniques, and engaged in post-interview recaps. They took their Shepherd role seriously by masterfully tailoring cover letters for job applications and writing thank-you notes after interviews. It was a painstaking process for Max and for his parents. They were fatigued and discouraged, and often worried that their son lacked the essential goods for the "real world."

Shepherd's are triggered by:

- Divergence from the Herd: They become anxious when their teen goes off-course. Rather than pursuing remediation or a more individualized learning plan, Carol and Jim kept Max with the herd.
- Perceived deficiency: Carol and Jim viewed Max's neurodiversity as a deficiency.Although they didn't want him to feel different or inferior to his peers, they still managed to project their shame and misinterpretations about his challenges onto him.

Common Shepherd Pitfalls:

- Their protectiveness inadvertently hinders their sheep.
- Carol and Jim had been intent on protecting Max from his challenges, and were determined not to let them limit him.
- They overlook the value of individual differences.
- Carol and Jim had not processed their anxieties about Max's learning challenges. Perceiving them as a hindrance, they had shepherded him through mainstream programs and prohibited the school from offering support.

- They view any divergence from the path as a deficiency. Carol and Jim viewed Max's neurodiversity as a deficiency. Although they didn't want him to feel different or inferior to his peers, they still managed to project their shame and misinterpretations about his challenges onto him.
- They emphasize "going along with the herd" rather than considering remediation or closer attention to individualized learning. Carol and Jim were invested in proving that Max was "on grade level" rather than availing him of opportunities to learn more about how he learned.
- Shepherds can be outcome-driven, focusing so much on the destination that they miss valuable growth opportunities in the process. They shepherd their children through childhood and adolescence until they arrive at the point where they are free to find their own pastures.

It was evident that Max hadn't acquired many of the essential attributes necessary for independent living: essential self-knowledge; the ability to self-direct; a reliable sense of judgment; and the capacity to accurately assess his progress. His parents were compelled to direct, supplement, and shepherd him through life, thwarting his development.

Jim and Carol's well-intended misinterpretation of Max's challenges prompted them to conceal them. Thus, Max had little understanding of his own learning-style differences and expressed minimal curiosity about them. For Max to develop some of these important life skills, his parents would need to connect to their own anxieties and develop new ways of managing them.

MEET CAROL AND JIM

Jim was a computer scientist with a penchant for numbers and a love of math. Intent on achieving success, he had denied himself his true desire—to be a math teacher—and had instead worked his way through the ranks of a large computer software corporation. He enjoyed the lifestyle this work afforded him, buying a home in the affluent town where they raised their children. He was proud to support the family, knowing his wife didn't need to work outside the home.

In contrast to their older daughter, who they described as bookish, focused, and self-driven, Max exhibited more learning challenges. Early in his school career, he was diagnosed with a language processing disorder, which concerned his parents. They were determined to not allow such a label to prevent his school progress, to not "disable" him.

Carol, a stay-at-home mother, offered Max every possible support to shepherd him through his childhood, including school. An admitted helicopter parent, she was on top of his schedule and assignments—"not because I want to, but because *I have to!*" She managed his time, edited his essays, quizzed him before tests—a practice she sustained throughout his college years. She was deeply involved in the school's parent association, and developed informal connections with school faculty.

These Shepherd parents kept Max on a tight leash for fear that he'd wander off and get lost. Relying on both the Shepherd and the herd, they believed their vulnerable son was incapable of "finding his own way."

It seemed that Max had grown accustomed to his parents' style. He readily accepted their directions, suggestions, and guidance—at least, on the surface.

WHO IS MAX?

It was evident to me that Max was unenthusiastic and detached from his job, and felt resigned to its inevitability. He assumed that this was the fate of all sheep. He'd say, "It's a good job—good experience and good benefits. Nobody gets a great job when they're first out of school." Clearly, it had never occurred to him that sheep could chart their own path. I realized that Max had never believed other viable options were available to him.

We decided to backtrack and examine the origins of his path. As a history major, he had always enjoyed history and writing, though was never quite sure what he would do with it. He considered teaching, although he couldn't imagine returning to a classroom. Besides, his parents strongly discouraged this career, seeing it as "impractical," especially for a man.

I frequently wondered if he ever entertained independent thoughts. And if so, where were they? During sessions, he repeated certain statements in a parroted way, often attributing them to his parents. "My dad says . . . " If I challenged him with "That's what your dad says; what do *you* think?" he'd say, "I agree with him," or "It's a good point."

Max was a good sheep, following the herd and his well-intended Shepherds. As a result, he had never been given the option to tune into himself. Max was going through the motions, following the script. Although he denied feeling anxious or depressed, he did seem lost. I poked and prodded in a different way, to find the real Max beneath the surface presentation. He needed guidance, but of a different kind. He needed to get to know himself, and to tune into his own voice. I suggested that rather than focusing our sessions on "surviving" his moody and demanding boss, we explore Max himself.

Through this process, Max formulated and articulated his feelings, thoughts, desires, and interests. While he knew that he hated the work he was doing, and had no aspirations to climb this particular corporate ladder, he claimed to have no idea of what kind of profession he might prefer, what kind of career would align with his unexamined self.

Yet, when he was given the space and encouragement, he revealed his long-standing passion for music. As he spoke, his face lit up, his demeanor lightened, and his voice took on authority and became enthusiastic.

THE MUSICIAN

Like many adolescents, Max had enjoyed music, finding great solace in writing his own poetic lyrics to express and manage his emerging and complicated teen emotions. He even saved his birthday money, bought a guitar, and taught himself the basics. Throughout his adolescence and young adulthood, his love and appreciation for music deepened. Without any true detectable "talent," however, Max's musical interests barely registered on his parents' radar. They naturally assumed this was a passing adolescent phase, or, at best, a longer-term hobby. After all, what teen *doesn't* fantasize about becoming a rock star?

Nonetheless, Max's passion and interest in music only grew. He regularly attended concerts, learned about and followed both popular and obscure bands, experimented with a range of genres, and even organized a garage band with several friends. And in college, he continued playing guitar, listening to music, and going to concerts.

Upon arriving in New York, he spent many evenings supporting emerging musical artists and performing at informal open-mic nights at bars and venues in other boroughs. Though unglamorous and far from his upper-middle-class suburban upbringings, he loved the music scene. Max developed relationships with many aspiring musicians who shared his passion and interests. He felt alive in this environment, with a real sense of belonging.

Though he fantasized about a career in music, he was fully aware of his parents' views on its impracticality: "A teenage pipe dream!" While they appreciated his love for music, they didn't see any talent or ability in him. Loath to set him up for failure, they supported his hobby, but discouraged him from furthering a more serious pursuit. In fact, its mere mention as a career path was verboten.

A CIRCUITOUS PATH

Throughout the next several months, Max's work situation became increasingly untenable. He was unable to meet deadlines or adhere to his boss's high expectations, and he grew more and more resentful of the corporate rigidity. He spent many of our sessions describing his dislike for corporate life and its incongruity with his personality. Max was admittedly and unbearably miserable, something he hadn't allowed himself to consider up until this point. Much to his parents' dismay, and disapproval, Max took a temporary leave of absence to reconsider and redefine *his* goals.

FINDING HIS VOICE

In therapy, Max relished his continued self-examination, lowering the volume of cultural expectations and tuning in more closely to himself. While he appreciated his parents' good intentions and the aspirations of many of his peers, he was discovering that his desires were different. Gradually, Max learned that he was less interested in the prestige or trappings—or misguided security—of corporate culture. He had no desire to climb the corporate ladder, to sit at a desk or attend company meetings. The direction this herd was heading in did not suit him.

In fact, he came to realize that the city's pace, congestion, and noise didn't suit him, either. He yearned for the tranquility of nature and space in which to be creative. He wanted to surround himself with like-minded people. He had no illusions about becoming a rock star; in fact, fame and travel did not appeal to him. He simply wanted a more music-centered life.

Upon visiting two friends from the New York City music scene who had moved to Denver, Colorado, Max found his home! The city offered him countless music opportunities with a slower, more affordable, outdoor life. He was drawn to this community, and began to devise an exit strategy for his corporate position. Max was going off script and off course, exploring directions which aligned with his interests and desires. Slowly, he was developing inner resources and motivations—a real drive and sense of direction.

PARENTS' ANXIETY SPIRAL

Max's plan to leave his corporate position and pursue his interest in music panicked his parents. The well-worn, predictable, and safe path which they had so painstakingly paved for him was eroding. They feared the thought of Max blindly traversing a music path, with which they had so little familiarity. They became increasingly anxious that they were "setting him up for failure"—the antithesis of their Shepherd guidelines, instincts, and practices.

The more Max considered these possibilities, the more anxious and critical his parents became. His desires flew in the face of every protective fiber in their parental bodies. Carol and Jim worried that he was running away—that he couldn't hack the pressures of adulthood, and that he would not succeed in this industry. They were desperate to protect him from rejection; they couldn't bear the pain of watching him struggle.

Max's parents explicitly communicated their disapproval and disappointment to him: "We didn't work this hard to get you a college education so you could live in a group home of musicians." Clearly, this this was not the life they would have chosen for him.

Shepherd anxiety is triggered by:

- The prospect of going off course, leaving the herd and getting lost: Max's parents were anxious that his learning differences would set him too far apart from his peers, making him seem inferior. They worried about the pace of his learning and maturation, so they stepped in and guided/directed him accordingly.
- Not fitting in with sheep, straying too far, or falling behind the cultural norms: Carol and Jim were uncomfortable with Max's pursuing a career in music, as they were less familiar and less comfortable with this industry. They feared that he would not be able to support himself and that he would experience rejection and failure; thus, they discouraged this pursuit.
- Perceived Vulnerability:The prospect of Max feeling inferior prompted his parents to preemptively compensate for his challenges.The prospect of their child experiencing negative feelings, particularly rejection.

Common Shepherd pitfalls:

- The Shepherd parent may minimize or devalue the mastery and competence their teen experiences through practicing an activity they value.
- The Shepherd may be so focused on the outcome of their teen's path that they overlook the essential and unexpected growth that takes place during the process.
- The Shepherd's path for their teen may be so linear that they lose sight of the value, growth, and skills which can develop while taking detours.
- Shepherds can be prone to binary thinking, such as "success vs. failure" and "ability vs. disability."

Shepherds manage their anxiety by:

- Preempting their teen's pain (and subsequently their own) by interfering in or redirecting the teen's process: Max's parents didn't think that Max had any real musical talent, and they feared he would experience rejection and disappointment. Thus, they attempted to guide him toward a corporate job.

- Using their own skills to ensure that their teen stays on course, even if this undermines the teen. They take charge and assume responsibility for the teen's challenges:Carol and Jim feared that Max's learning differences would slow his academic and social progress, so they did everything in their power to remediate this. They tried to compensate for his perceived inadequacies, proofreading or doing his work for him, offering unsolicited solutions, suggestions, or advice in response to his work challenges.
- Defining the right course according to what they think is best for their teen: Max's parents believed that a corporate position was the most secure and responsible professional route, and they guided Max in that direction. They assumed they knew what was best for their teen and didn't encourage or trust his own exploration (unwittingly depriving him of exercising essential developmental muscles).

Shepherd Thought Distortions:

- Minimization: Max's parents minimized his strengths and overlooked his skills, abilities and interests.
- Jumping to Conclusions: Carol and Jim assumed that if Max strayed off course, he would not be able to succeed.
- Belief Bias: Max's parents had many preconceived and inaccurate perceptions of Max's neurodiversity.

SHIFTING FOCUS TO THEMSELVES

As Carol and Jim became more aware of their anxieties and the ways they were interfering with Max's development, they realized that the path they had defined for him was not leading him toward a happier and more successful future. They realized that they needed to respond to Max, rather than react to their own anxieties. As they did so, they were able to reframe their understanding of Max's learning differences, his developmental needs, and his acquisition of life skills in accordance with his intentions. They realized that there was developmental value in the risks he was taking, in his defining and exploring uncharted territory, developing a sense of agency and ownership of his process.

And with their shift in course, Max was beginning to develop essential skills for adulthood. For the first time, he was planning, budgeting, and figuring out how to make ends meet. He was trusting his judgment, learning from his experience, and redirecting himself as needed. Gradually, Max was developing his own professional connections and an inner resourcefulness that he could rely on throughout life. Perhaps most importantly, he was experiencing a sense of mastery from pursuing self-directed goals and aspirations.

Carol and Jim realized that perhaps Max was not escaping the conventional path, but rather connecting to himself. And he was teaching and guiding them in a new way!

HEARING MAX'S VOICE

Carol and Jim could not deny the more motivated, engaged, and responsible adult emerging before them—not rebelling against them, but in accordance with himself. As he considered this less traditional linear job track, he was assuming more agency over his life. And he was obviously enjoying the sense of belonging and community among similarly minded peers.

Without their connections, he networked with other creatives in a way that he had never done before—practicing his pitch, experimenting with styles of engagement, and exploring possibilities and options that he had never considered before—acquiring skills that would help him in the long term, self-directed and financially responsible.

He interviewed at a local music store and signed up to teach guitar to younger children, allowing him to devote his energies to his music and to perform at night. He learned to live more affordably, devising a budget and picking up extra work when needed. Part of this maturation required his identifying these needs, including the kind of support he needed from his parents. With a well-thought-out budget, he requested a nominal subsidy from them for one year.

THE NEW LANDSCAPE

Like Max, his parents were assuming a new challenge as well. They were recognizing and tolerating the anxieties that arose within them. They encouraged Max to make decisions and plans, and served as sounding boards rather than directors or critics, finding ways to promote his "thinking through" processes and outcomes. Carol and Jim challenged their binary thinking. They redefined their notion of success, seeing it as a process of Max acquiring internal skills, through his own experience. They challenged their preexisting beliefs about his learning challenges and conventional definitions of success, and they resisted the urge to forecast—to think too far into the future—and to stay in the moment with Max.

Gradually, Max's parents' disappointment morphed into admiration for their son's enthusiasm—his excitement, liveliness, and sense of hope. Although idealistic and possibly unrealistic, they were proud of Max's willingness to take risks, respect himself, tune into his own voice, and drown out the voices that he had been acculturated into. As he listened to himself, he gauged and fine-tuned his desires, his goals, his aspirations—how he felt most content. And while there were certainly bumps in the road as they all traversed a new path—in their relationship, and in Max's sense of self and confidence—they knew they were ultimately moving together toward a new and expanded success.

Chapter 10

Gina the Corrector

When I greeted Gina in the waiting room, she forced a courteous smile. Precariously juggling her iPhone, shopping bags, and purse, she walked toward the office. It was evident that our session occupied one hour of her precisely organized morning routine of exercise, errands, and appointments, a to-do list that needed to be completed before the three p.m. school pickup. She hurried to the couch, placing her cell phone facedown beside her as usual, and neatly draping her Lululemon sweatshirt over her bags, which she aligned with the couch frame. While settling in and redoing the elastic around her loose bun, she downloaded the week's frustrations. She was determined to cover every issue on her therapy agenda, starting with her husband.

"He criticizes me constantly. Every step I make related to the kids, he comments on. He's stifling my maternal instincts. I wish he'd stay in his own lane!"

As the mother of three children ages nine to eighteen, and married for eighteen years, Gina and Barry shared a full and busy family life. Until their oldest daughter, Delaney, had reached adolescence, the couple had been a well-oiled partnership of teamwork and responsibilities. But the challenges and pressures of parenting a high school student had shifted their parenting dynamic considerably. They disagreed about everything from curfews and skirt lengths to study habits, homework load, and grades.

"How are we supposed to present a united front to Delaney when we can't agree among ourselves?" she said.

"What happened?" I asked.

"I logged into the school grading system yesterday and found out that Delaney hadn't handed in *three* of her AP Bio assignments." She held up three fingers to emphasize her point. "Is she kidding me? This is a kid who wants to get into a top-tier pre-med program. She could have the highest test scores in the class, but if she doesn't hand in her work, her grades will plummet. Homework is fifty percent of her grade!" Gina's anger veiled her underlying panic.

"I was furious," she continued. "We give her so many privileges—camp, vacations, concerts. All we ask is that she does well in school. But when I texted Barry to tell him what I'd found out, he criticized my logging into the site in the first place. He accused me of being intrusive and overinvolved. I didn't even tell him I'd already emailed her teacher because that would have only fueled his fire!"

"You wanted to feel like you were on the same team, but you got criticized instead," I said.

Gina nodded, her eyes shiny as she held back furious tears. "This is the new us. He is so concerned about my being overly involved that he automatically takes the opposing position. He's more interested in disagreeing with me than in our daughter's future!"

Gina's devotion to her daughter and worries about Delaney's sudden lack of motivation were totally understandable. Like any loving parent, Gina was concerned about her daughter's disinterest in school and what that meant for her future. However, from where I sat, I strongly suspected that something else was going on.

Delaney had been a typical firstborn—highly responsible, hardworking, and ambitious. Since her earliest days of school, Gina had appreciated her daughter's studiousness and was inspired and gratified by Delaney's long-held desire to become a doctor. Gina was determined to help her daughter achieve this goal by making connections for internships and helping her apply for prestigious research opportunities. Until this point, Delaney had seemed on track to becoming a viable candidate for a selective pre-med program.

While Delaney did not necessarily need Gina's vigilance and oversight of her schoolwork, Gina always kept her finger on the pulse, keeping close tabs on her grades and closely tracking the statistics, rankings, and admissions criteria of selective programs. After all, this was the role of a supportive, attentive, and loving mother, helping her daughter fulfill her lifelong dream. And Gina was intent on being right beside her daughter, if not ahead of her, all the way.

Gina's deep disappointment and incredulity over what she described as her daughter's recent laziness and irresponsibility overshadowed the deeper anxiety stirring beneath the surface. Gina was determined to prevent her daughter from derailing any further. Given the increasing competitiveness of reputable pre-med programs, Gina knew that every test, every grade, and every course could impact Delaney's trajectory. Her daughter (and she!) could not afford any missteps, so Gina tightened the parental reins, grounding her, lecturing her, and closely monitoring her assignments.

And as often happens, the more anxious and out of control Gina felt, the more overbearing and intrusive she became. This, in turn, prompted Delaney's resistance and resentment. Clearly, this was not the outcome that either desired.

In order for Gina to be responsive and truly helpful to her daughter, she needed to reexamine the emotions engendered in her, particularly her anxiety. In the process of doing so, she was reminded of her own deep-seated and painful thwarted ambitions from her history, experiences she was determined not to replicate with her own children.

"Are you worried that what happened to you will happen to her?" I inquired gently.

With tears slowly running down her cheeks, Gina delved into her story.

WHO ARE CORRECTORS?

While all parents reflect on their histories, Correctors use what they've learned from their past to manage their fear of repeating the same experience for their teen. By keeping their challenging past in mind (both consciously and unconsciously), they attempt to prevent recurrences of past pain and disappointments from their own childhood. Correctors attempt to assuage their childhood pain by providing the reverse childhood experience for their own children, to the best of their ability. Latchkey children become stay-at-home parents; children raised in strict homes become permissive parents; and children of quick-tempered parents become conflict-avoidant adults. As they parent their own children, they reverse or correct the painful elements of their past.

Correctors draw direct connections between painful childhood experiences and their parents' "errors"—lack of attunement, misguidedness, or outright failures. By providing their own children with a vastly different, often opposite parenting approach, they offer themselves a corrective experience. This negative bias against their own experiences informs many of their parenting decisions, particularly regarding achievement.

Correctors have a negative association with their past, particularly the interplay between their parents' attitudes toward achievement and what they experienced in childhood. They have devised a narrative (unconscious or conscious) about their relationship with achievement growing up, and their parents' role in it. They use their childhood experience as a guide for what *not* to do, because their decisions and perspectives are informed by their own parents' errors. Correctors try to have a corrective experience by offering their children a better experience than what they had as children.

GINA'S STORY

For as long as Gina could remember, she had been studious and focused. As a child, she spent hours in her room writing elaborate stories and immersing herself in literature. Her affinity for words led her to become the chief editor of her high school literary magazine and lead writer for her school newspaper. She dreamt of becoming a writer for *The New Yorker* someday, and was working hard to be accepted to a private college that many of her writer role models had attended.

The time Gina spent writing, reading, and editing also served as a respite from the challenges at home. Her father, an adoring and charismatic man, had cancer. No longer able to work, he had sold his deteriorating orthodontics practice to a colleague. Gina's mother was struggling to manage her day-to-day responsibilities and was under intense pressure to pay the mounting medical and family bills. Throughout this difficult time, Gina kept her acceptance to the college of her dreams as her North Star.

Tragically, Gina's father passed away several weeks prior to her acceptance to the college she'd worked so hard to attend. Overwhelmed and grief-stricken, her mother became fixated on finances, convinced that she was unable to afford the university's tuition. She insisted that Gina attend a less expensive school. So as not to burden her mother further, Gina readily complied.

The inability to go to the college she believed would set her on a path toward becoming a successful writer triggered a domino effect of thwarted ambitions throughout the rest of Gina's adulthood. Fearful of replicating her family's financial instability, she accepted a position at an established marketing firm after graduation and buried her writing aspirations in favor of a seemingly more practical and "safe" profession.

This unresolved loss became a conscious and unconscious force behind Gina's parenting decisions with Delaney. On some level, by facilitating Delaney's path to success, Gina hoped to heal the wounds of her own lost career aspirations. Gina's worry about replicating the problems of her past put her parental achievement anxiety in the driver's seat.

THE CORRECTOR'S DILEMMA

Gina was anxious about Delaney's decline in school performance, which manifested in conflict with her husband and resentment toward her daughter, further distancing her relationship with Delaney. She was desperate to ensure that her daughter had every opportunity possible and didn't want her to suffer like she had. Gina wanted to be an involved, supportive, and encouraging mother to help her daughter achieve her potential. She couldn't bear to watch her daughter feel the regret that she herself had experienced in adolescence.

UNDERSTANDING CORRECTOR ANXIETY

Correctors are disheartened by their past, the particularities of the ways they were parented. They are tuned into the misgivings and detriments of pivotal childhood experiences and parental messaging, and they are determined to offer the antithetical experiences for their own children.

As parents, Correctors are anxious about the prospect of replicating their own parents' errors. Thus, they deliberately counter their painful childhood experiences by providing the opposite for their own children.

Corrector anxiety is triggered by:

- The prospect of replicating the pain they experienced in childhood, and/or repeating what they view as their parents' parenting mistakes.
- Feeling powerless to reverse the trajectory of their unresolved pain from childhood.
- Seeing the prospect of similar negative outcomes that they experienced growing up.

The Corrector parent deals with their anxiety by:

- Making decisions for their children based on their own experiences and reactions.
- Attempting to heal their childhood pain by offering their own children the opposite experience.
- Ensuring that they do not repeat painful patterns from their past.

THE ANXIETY SPIRAL

Gina was determined to be as attentive to Delaney's achievements as possible. Unlike her own mother, who had been overwhelmed by the financial and emotional demands of single motherhood, Gina was intentional and involved in her daughter's academics. She wanted her daughter to feel well supported, not alone and left to her own devices, the way she had felt when her father became ill. The more Delaney withdrew her efforts in school, the more vigilant and involved Gina became. Unfortunately, this backfired.

Common Corrector pitfalls:

- They try to correct their challenging childhood through how they parent their own teen.

- They project their own feelings and needs onto their teen. They have difficulty seeing or tolerating differences between themselves and their children.
- They allow their own history to blind them to their teen's needs.
- They oversimplify how their history contributed to their current achievements.

FACING THE ANXIETY

In our sessions, we unpacked three main cognitive distortions that were governing how Gina was thinking about Delaney's behavior and future and driving her anxiety spiral:

1. **Binary thinking:** Gina was determined to offer her daughter a different experience than what she had had growing up. Her mother had been unavailable and uninvolved, so Gina intentionally became what she saw as the only other, opposite option: extremely available and involved.
2. **Blaming:** Gina was burdened by her thwarted and unfulfilled professional ambitions. She drew a direct link between her mother's unavailability during her adolescence and her regret. She blamed her mother for the derailment of her professional trajectory.
3. **Catastrophic thinking:** The prospect of Delaney not achieving her goals reignited many of Gina's painful memories from her past. She feared that if Delaney did not get into a leading pre-med program, she would endure the regret and dissatisfaction that had been plaguing Gina throughout her adulthood.

As we identified Gina's anxious thought patterns, she became better equipped to challenge them. She did so by using the perks of the Corrector PART.

Corrector Perks:

- They're naturally self-reflective.
- They're able to make connections between the past and present.

- They're aware of how their history has contributed to their current achievements.
- They're able to change the story they tell themselves about their past.

As Gina reflected more deeply on her past and clarified her values, she realized how her fears of replicating her childhood pain were steering her further away from fulfilling Delaney's needs. This invaluable insight illuminated the many differences between her own past and her daughter's present, and allowed her to see the situation with clarity and perspective.

HEALING THE CORRECTOR'S WOUNDS

Over our next few sessions, Gina came to realize that Delaney's college application process had reopened painful memories of her mother's unavailability and of Gina's deep regret over her career. Expressing great sadness during our sessions helped her to separate her experience from Delaney's.

Gina shared the nuances and complexities of her painful history with Barry—not just the headlines, but her deep-seated fears that Delaney would feel as unsupported and adrift as she had felt as a teen. Barry, in turn, appreciated the origins of her anxieties and agreed to compassionately support her as they navigated this stressful parenting time together. His understanding of his wife's adolescent pain and her efforts to protect her daughter from pain allowed them to renegotiate their approach to Delaney. When Gina's anxiety rose and she was tempted to meddle, Barry validated her anxiety and suggested a pause before taking action. This improved their relationship and united their approach toward Delaney.

Gina and Barry's renewed perspective, mitigated reactivity, and decreased family tension created emotional space and safety for Delaney to be more expressive and direct with them. Through more open conversations, Delaney revealed that she might have chosen medicine because she didn't want to disappoint her parents, especially because both of her grandfathers had been doctors. In fact, she had become interested in politics and social justice. She acknowledged that she may have tried to fail science so that she didn't have to tell them she didn't want to go to medical school anymore. Without the grades, the decision would be made for her.

It must be noted that trying to work through the past doesn't always work. The Corrector's absorption in the past may prevent them from recognizing their teens' unique needs and personalities. Being a Corrector becomes problematic when they're unable to separate their past from their teen's present. This focus on the past can cause them to make decisions based on what their wounded teen self needs rather than on what their own child needs. Like a person on a diet who prepares delicious treats for others to satisfy their own cravings, the opportunities the Corrector gives to their teen may be more about the parent's needs than their child's.

These aren't easy changes to make. The stories we tell ourselves about our past can be so deeply embedded that there will be many times when we won't even realize that we're trying to fix what didn't work for us rather than respond to the emotional needs and individuality of our children.

Gina was able to become the supportive and available parent that she wanted to be by becoming more aware of her efforts to reverse—or at least not reenact—the traumas from her past. Her exploration and understanding of her history enabled her to deepen her relationship with her husband, and to view Delaney as a separate individual with her own needs and desires, responding to her accordingly—a mutually beneficial outcome.

Chapter 11

Nathan the Replicator

Mary and Nathan referred their thirteen-year-old son, Cory, to therapy because he was becoming increasingly irritable and combative at home. Since the summer before eighth grade, Cory had become quick to anger, intolerant of his siblings, and oppositional toward them. They were bothered by his negative attitude and believed that he had alienated himself almost entirely from the family.

Though I anticipated meeting a resistant and resentful teen in my waiting room, I was greeted by a friendly, confident boy. He quickly rose from his chair, outstretched his arm to shake my hand, and held the wheels of his skateboard with the other. Cory was a tall, lanky teen with long, sweeping dirty-blond bangs and baggy, skater-style clothes. His wide grin revealed a mouthful of colorful braces.

Cory readily engaged, seemed eager to talk, and was adept at expressing his frustrations and describing his annoyances with his parents. Both insightful and self-aware, he offered his detailed observations, perceptions, and interpretations of the family dynamics. Basically, he said, "I'm the black sheep in my family. Everyone knows it. My parents want me to see you to get fixed. I'm thinking this might be a good opportunity to fix them," he added, laughing.

The middle child of three boys, Cory had struggled to find his place in the family. He viewed his older brother, Chris, as a mirror image of his parents, particularly his father. "Chris is exactly the kind of kid they always wanted. He gets great grades and is captain of the lacrosse team," he explained resentfully, "just like my dad." And according to him, his younger brother, Chase, fit the family mold as well.

Cory, on the other hand, was a technological whiz who created elaborate movies and visuals on his computer. He spent hours designing and editing graphics. Media rather than words helped him to express his true self. His gifts were what set him apart in his family, both positively and negatively. While Cory's parents often enjoyed his sense of humor and out-of-the-box thinking, they resented his outspokenness and "snarky" tone.

Unfortunately, being different didn't work well in this family. Instead, it made them anxious. In Cory's telling, Nathan and Mary expected all of their children to attend the New England boarding school that they and their relatives had gone to for generations, a revered institution with a reputation for having a direct path to the most elite colleges. It was understood that going to this school was "just what our family does."

But as Cory's middle school years ended, he outright refused the family plan. He insisted that he wanted to go to the neighborhood public school, which had an excellent technology department that far exceeded what the boarding school had to offer. The more Nathan and Mary pushed Cory to attend their alma mater, the angrier he became. Their family was at a standstill.

"Look at me! Could you imagine *me* at some preppy school wearing a blue blazer with a school crest on the pocket, khakis, and fancy shoes? Really?"

Frustrated by his parents' refusal to listen to him, Cory hoped I would advocate on his behalf. "Maybe if you talk to them, they'll believe you," he pleaded. "They sure as hell don't care what I have to say." Like many teenagers, Cory felt devalued and minimized. As a result, he increased the frequency and intensity of his complaints.

I agreed to meet with his parents.

WHO ARE REPLICATORS?

In previous chapters we have examined the many cognitive distortions and their origins, particularly deep-seated beliefs. The notion that "This is the way things are," or "This is the way we do things" can be so ingrained in our psyches that we don't even recognize that it's a worldview. These beliefs are so fundamental to our thinking that we view them as facts, and we construct our lives, and our children's lives, around them.

This is the central attribute of Replicator parents. They've internalized their experiences from childhood, and with or without consideration, they have decided to perpetuate them. They've come to believe that the way their family operates is simply "the way it's done." Often, they do so without evaluating, considering, or questioning why. Their own parents' methods, style, and actions worked for them, and they have minimal reason to examine them further.

As a result, these norms not only become intertwined with the psychology of Replicators, part of their standard mode of operation, but they also attach unconscious meaning and interpretations to these actions. For example, a Replicator parent assigns chores to their child, believing "Children help around the house. It's part of being a respectful, responsible family member." Yet, another family might approach tasks the opposite way: "I take care of my children by performing household chores. It is my responsibility as the parent to do so." Different families, different belief systems, different parenting behaviors—all woven into the fabric of the family's norms.

Often, it's not until we live with someone from another family—a college roommate, a housemate, a significant other or spouse—that we begin to identify and question the many norms by which our family of origin and others live. Norms become so embedded in the family's functioning that they're taken for granted. One's family communication style, daily ways of operating, and habits become so routine and expected that they are rarely questioned or even noticed.

Replicators are motivated by what is familiar and has worked in the past. They are not seeking change or difference. They may update or improve existing parenting behaviors, but they embrace tradition, customs, and maintaining what's familiar.

Most parents unknowingly replicate experiences from their past—making a treasured recipe for a holiday meal or perpetuating a family tradition become automatically integrated into their current family's functioning. These are ways of maintaining continuity between generations and replicating that to which they've become accustomed.

With the best of intentions, Replicators believe they possess the formula for success for their own teens. They may often reference their history as a benchmark for normalcy, saying things like, "This is how I did it." While this can sometimes be beneficial, if their teen wants to take a different route, Replicators' parental achievement anxiety about an unfamiliar life path can interfere with their ability to see their child's needs clearly.

Asking your teen to follow the same path you took simplifies what can often be complicated and multilayered parenting decisions—understandably attractive. For Replicators, it can be stressful when they don't understand the road their teen wants to take, and stress can increase parental achievement anxiety. It's natural to want to steer one's child in a direction that increases parental comfort.

Characteristics of Replicator anxiety:

- Replicators maintain traditions and styles and view them as "right."
- They appreciate continuity between generations, and foster it by "maintaining" the practices, explicit and implicitly.
- They view their childhoods positively; are less critical of them; or they have not examined their histories at all. This may be reflective of their not emotionally separating from their parents.
- Replicators are more likely to conform, accept norms of familiar systems, and internalize family norms as truths.
- They may be more likely to resist change, even considering change to be a personal rejection of their character.
- They become anxious by suggestions of change or by challenges made to existing systems they have deemed as successful.

MEET NATHAN

Nathan was a tall, handsome man in his mid-forties. Regularly dressed in a precisely pressed suit, his crisp white shirt with cuffs bearing his initials had the straight-out-of-central-casting appearance of a New York City attorney, and he was well groomed for the part. His dark brown hair neatly parted to the side, tortoiseshell glasses, and pronounced jawline enhanced his professional presentation. Even when I met them at the end of a workday, he maintained his well-polished, seemingly untouched appearance. Yet, despite his somewhat formal presentation, he was warm, engaging, and personable.

As one of the youngest associates to have been named partner at his white-shoe law firm, Nathan was a dedicated attorney who viewed his achievements as the reward for his sixty-plus-hour workweeks and relentless ambition. He attributed his strong work ethic, professionalism, and success to the qualities that had been instilled in him by his parents and older siblings.

The youngest of his parents' four children, he dutifully followed in his family's footsteps. As a devoted student and athlete, he mimicked his father's and older brothers' academic and athletic trajectories, and took great pride in doing so. He described his traditional upbringing, noting its predictably structured rhythm: dinner served at six p.m. each night, family attendance at church every Sunday, and summer vacations on Cape Cod.

Nathan's father, also an attorney, was the product of the family's pedigreed education. A busy man with community obligations and a high-pressure career, he was not involved in the day-to-day functioning of the household. His parents' roles were clearly defined. And while Nathan hadn't spent as much time with his father, he had always looked up to him. For as long as he could remember, he'd admired his father's discipline and intellect, and "how well he had provided for our family." While he had never articulated it explicitly, Nathan had automatically modeled his adult life after his parents.

THE REPLICATOR DILEMMA

During our initial parent sessions, Nathan hesitantly admitted that he worried about Cory's "unconventionality" and refusal to follow the family path. "I just don't get him," he admitted. "Of course, I love him because he's my son, but he is kind of quirky—like he needs to march to the beat of his own drum about *everything*. He throws a monkey wrench into every plan we have. At some point, he'll have to learn to follow along, not keep making up his own rules."

It was inconceivable to Nathan that his son wouldn't want to attend the school that had been the family tradition for generations. "You should see this place—it's idyllic! One of the most beautiful campuses imaginable, and my siblings and I got an incredible education and made our closest lifelong friends there. But I can't *force* him to go if he refuses!"

As Nathan vacillated between frustration and sadness, he readily accepted my suggestion that we meet individually to discuss this in greater detail.

FACING REPLICATOR ANXIETY

As Nathan entered my office the following week, he placed his briefcase beside him and began with his usual pleasantries. Clearly immersed in the culture of politeness and formality, he seemed to need time to "warm up" before diving into his more vulnerable feelings.

Finally, after several minutes, I gently picked up where we had previously left off.

"I've been thinking about how tough it is when our kids are so different from us. And Cory seems to operate *so* differently than you, on so many levels," I said.

"On *every* level! And this school thing is really becoming a problem," he confirmed, shaking his head with annoyance.

"You have such positive associations to the school, and you want Cory to have a similarly positive experience there. I imagine that it's hard to have your son so outrightly reject something that is so special and meaningful to you," I reflected.

"Boarding school is the best experience for teenagers, and this school offers everything to make it so. They know teenagers better than anyone—how they learn, what they need, and how to treat them—better than most parents, and definitely better than any public school could do!"

"It's inconceivable to you that someone, even a teenager, wouldn't be able to appreciate this. So, what could Cory's hesitancy be about?" I asked.

"Just to be contrarian—to reject what we expect him to do," Nathan said. Certain of his interpretation, he continued. "And that's even more reason to send him there. If he's going to spend his time in our home criticizing or disagreeing with what we want him to do, you'd think he'd be dying to leave! It's impossible not to love that place. My best memories and friends are from there. They're like a second family!"

As Nathan described the many times Cory had rejected the family norms, his frustration became more palpable. "I wish he'd just do what we told him to do. I am so tired of fighting with him—trying to *convince* him to do what he should! I win more cases at work than I do with my own son!" he said sarcastically.

As he described his frustrations, tears began to well in his eyes.

"It's hard to feel like you can't get through to him," I said. "A powerless kind of feeling?"

"Yes, which seems like some kind of weird role reversal," Nathan said. "I'm the parent, and I'm begging him to consider what I *know* is best for him! I never would have challenged my parents this way. What my dad said went. We didn't second-guess his every direction. We knew what was expected and we did what we were supposed to. And it worked. We all graduated from really good schools, and a lot of that had to do with the boarding school. They call it a prep school for a reason— it completely prepared all of us for college," Nathan said passionately.

"The school is an integral part of your identity, something you hold close to your heart, as does your whole family—your dad, your siblings, your grandfather. I wonder if his rejection of the school feels like a rejection of you," I said.

Sitting back on the couch, he paused, contemplating this possibility.

Reluctant to break his thought process, I added, "It's very important to you, and Cory is important to you. And since you love your son, you want to share it with him. For him to have the positive experience that you and your siblings had—that's what loving parents want," I validated.

"Are you saying that maybe I want him to go so badly because I love him, and if he doesn't want to go, I'll feel hurt and insulted—like a failure?"

"I don't know. How do you imagine you'd feel if he were not to go there?"

"I'm not sure . . . I *do* know that my entire extended family would be dismayed, wondering if there was something wrong with him. My dad especially wouldn't get it."

As we proceeded to explore the dynamics of his relationship with his father—Nathan's pride, admiration, and idealization of him—it became increasingly evident that he had only reflected on this through a positive lens. He had never allowed himself to view his father through his own adult lens; it had previously made him too anxious. Until now, he had towed the family's party line that their family was, in many ways, "perfect."

"And as you imagine sharing this with them, and you imagine their judgments, how do you feel?"

"To say that I feel like a failure is too strong of a word. I guess I'd be embarrassed, ashamed—like I'd have to couch it in a lot of disclaimers. I don't want them to look down on Cory. He'd be the first kid of all the cousins not to go there!"

"You worry that others won't understand him. He is different from you and from your family in many ways. He's a pretty talented and unique kid, with many gifts and abilities that are different from what you're accustomed to, perhaps from the qualities your family valued when you were growing up."

"It's funny that you say that. I had a really good friend who was an incredible drummer—kind of a rebel, but super-talented. When we hung out, I used to play around on his drum kit, and it was so much fun. Maybe that's how I got out my teen angst! But when I asked my parents if I could take it up, they summarily refused. They didn't want the noise in our house, or to encourage this 'rock music stuff'! I always regretted not having taken it up. I'm pretty into music, and I think I could have been a pretty good drummer."

"It's hard when parents shut down parts of their kids that make them uncomfortable. We are all creatures of habit and resist change. And teenagers are all about change!"

Nathan nodded in agreement.

"It sounds like Cory is clear about what he wants to try, what he's interested in applying himself toward. It may be different from others in your family, but it's what he enjoys. Might there be value to exploring his desires? How might he respond?"

"I think that he'd feel great," Nathan said. "The most respected and understood that he's felt in a long time."

UNDERSTANDING THE REPLICATOR'S ANXIETY

Replicators reflect positively on their childhoods and have internalized their family experiences. When they become parents themselves, they strongly identify with their own parents and try to live up to the standards they set, leading to thought patterns like "This is what a father does." So, when a child calls any of that into question or resists a norm, Replicators may feel threatened or anxious, causing them to resist difference. Navigating unfamiliar territory is more anxiety-producing than replicating the familiarity, security, and comfort of the past.

Replicator anxiety is triggered by:

- Unfamiliarity, newness, or change.
- Uncertainty or questioning of existing systems that have always worked for them.
- Departure from the success formula with which they're familiar.
- Perceived criticisms of their past, or their own parents.

Replicators deal with their anxiety by:

- Rigid adherence to traditions from the past.
- Unconsciously and consciously repeating patterns from their family of origin.
- Resisting further examination of their relationship with their parents or objective examination of their past.
- Projecting their own feelings and needs onto their teen.
- Having difficulty seeing or tolerating differences between themselves and their children.
- Allowing their history to blind them to their teen's needs.
- Oversimplifying how their history contributed to their current achievements.

The more they are called into question, the more defensive they become. Unlike the Corrector who tries to reverse their childhood experiences, Replicators perceive their being asked to examine their history as a criticism of them and/or their parents. They experience change as threatening and fearsome, and this catalyzes the Replicator's anxiety spiral.

Replicator perks:

- Satisfaction with/positive experiences with achievement.

- They are relatively "unconflicted" internally; they reflect positively on their upbringing, and they view their parents through a positive lens.
- They uphold family traditions and values, maintaining continuity and connection between generations.
- They have an enhanced sense of "belonging" within the family due to shared values and practices.

Common Replicator thought distortions:

- Overgeneralization: They attribute their current success to one factor.
- Black-and-white thinking: "My experience was the right way; that which is unfamiliar is wrong or too risky."

Common Replicator Pitfalls:

- Depriving themselves and their children of opportunities to explore uncharted territory.
- Lack of deeper exploration of values/beliefs; rigid adherence to deeper-seated beliefs.

ACCEPTING DIFFERENCES

As Nathan took a step back to explore the "whys" of his parenting behavior, he realized that his unexamined conviction to repeat the past had blinded him to the gifts of the present. As he availed himself of the unexamined aspects of his own history and personality, he opened up to Cory, appreciating his son's talents, interests, passion, and his courage to be different. Nathan was better able to embrace Cory more fully, rather than perceiving Cory's individuality as a rejection of him.

With a renewed acceptance, Nathan identified his desire to connect with his son, and committed to spending time to allow Cory to teach him, not only about his movies, but about himself. By virtue of his son's introduction, Nathan reconnected to his previously undeveloped interest in movies and cinematography. Together, they watched movies, both conventional and obscure. As Cory shared his expertise and knowledge on the topic, Nathan learned not only about movies, but about unrealized parts of himself.

As their connection grew, Nathan began to accept Cory for who he was, rather than who he thought he should be. He was able to really hear for the first time how much Cory wanted to attend public school, as well as take classes at a nearby film school in New York City. Additionally, and more importantly, Nathan and Mary realized that Cory's living at home for high school would give them more opportunities to spend time with him, something they valued even more deeply than professional achievement.

They decided to allow Cory to go to the local school, where his interests and passions would be nurtured, rather than force him to conform to the family tradition of attending the elite boarding school. This was an important learning experience for the family, and led to greater harmony for all.

Chapter 12

PART III: Putting It All Together

The Value of Values

I often begin parenting roundtables, lectures, and workshops by asking parents, "What is most important to you as a parent? What makes you feel like a 'successful' parent?"

Invariably, 90 percent of parents' responses include versions of "I just want my kids to be happy" and "I want them to be fulfilled and functioning members of society," along with a smattering of "I want them to reach their full potential, or become their best selves." A common refrain has also been "I don't need them to go to Harvard or be an Olympic athlete. I just want them to be the best they can be."

Valuing our kids' happiness and fulfillment is a nearly universal parenting experience, and the identification of these parenting values is helpful, at least in theory. But how do we put these values into practice? What do they look like in our everyday parenting? How do we convey these values to our children, aligning what we say with what we do? The value of "just wanting them to be happy and fulfilled" often gets lost in the translation into action. While this is what we truly want for them, we lose sight of it in our daily functioning. Happiness and fulfillment are difficult to measure, so "I want the best for you" often translates to "Get better grades, aim for higher scores, and keep your eye on college admissions."

But research indicates that there is no correlation between college selectivity and student happiness.[1] And not once in my thirty-year practice have I heard a child tell me that their parents' pressure on them to succeed has made them happier or more fulfilled. Most teenagers believe that their parents want them to make a lot of money or attend "the best school possible."[2] As parents emphasize grades, scores, and rankings, students learn to see prestigious internships, acceptance into top-tier colleges, and receiving awards as being more important than their personal happiness or fulfillment.[3] Clearly, there's a disconnect here between parental values and action.

For the record, there is a link between achievement and happiness, but not in the way that many of us emphasize in daily life. We experience fulfillment, competence, and mastery from *measured* challenges. Similar to strength training in the gym, gradually increasing weight and challenging muscles makes them stronger; a little soreness is an indication of growth. Yet, increasing weight too quickly (particularly to keep up with or exceed what the weightlifter beside us can do) leads to the inability to function the following day, or worse, injury or longer-term damage to the body.

As it turns out, values are only of value when we can see them in action. Good intentions mean nothing when we act against them (inadvertently or not). Actually *defining* our values, in a way that translates into behavior, is more difficult than we think. We may have an internal "knowing" of what's most important to us—"I want my kids to be happy and fulfilled"—but it is the actionable articulation of our values that allows us to align our behavior with them. We need to first define our values and then reflect on how to behave in accordance with those values.

WHAT ARE VALUES?

In his book *The Road to Character*, David Brooks[4] highlights "eulogy character virtues." What do we want people to say about us when we die? Those are the qualities that truly matter. I have yet to hear a eulogy include "He got a 1500 on his SATs"; "She was accepted to nine out of ten colleges she applied to"; or "His boss gave him a lot of promotions and raises." It is the attributes and qualities that we value of the person being eulogized that we speak about in such instances. These are the types of values we want to "dig into" in this chapter.

From a psychological perspective, our values are pillars of our identity. They are the qualities of being and doing that reflect our true authentic selves (see figure 1).

Let's unpack that a bit. The true self[5] is the way we are in our most private moments. It's emblematic of who we feel we are, and is the part of us that remains continuous throughout our lives. Our true selves are not our carefully crafted social personalities but rather what is formed through experience and, along with our values, are not consciously chosen by us. Nonetheless, they are what we think of when we think of ourselves. When we behave in ways that don't align with our true selves we feel discomfort, guilt, and/or inner conflict. When we are acting in ways that don't align with our true selves, we are unable to feel centered or at peace. Defining our values in words allows us to be more intentional about aligning our actions and behaviors with our true selves.

This is what we witnessed again and again in the PARTs chapters. We saw parents acting in accordance with their anxiety rather than their values. This threw them into direct conflict with their kids, or internal conflict with themselves. It was only through taking a step back and recentering themselves in their values that they were able to adjust their behavior and find resolution with their children and themselves.

A few other important things to note about values:

- Values cannot be right or wrong; they are highly individual.
- When we identify a value, it doesn't mean we don't have other, even seemingly contradictory values that we have not yet identified.
- The way we define our values can change throughout life as we evolve and navigate different developmental stages. (For example, when I was young I valued freedom, which translated into "not being pinned down," but as I grew older I redefined that same value as self-expression, which was possible even when I decided to settle down and choose a career and life partner.)
- Adolescents internalize their parents' values throughout adolescence and also reject them as they emotionally separate and develop their own identities. (Translation: Whether or not they show/admit it, parental values are very influential on teens.)

HOW DO WE ALIGN OUR BEHAVIOR
WITH OUR VALUES?

STEP 1: Identify your dilemma (what decision you are struggling with)

In the appendix, you'll find a complete worksheet that walks you through the steps of identifying your values and how to act on those values when making a parenting decision.

The first step is to identify what dilemma or decision you are currently struggling with. Maybe you've had something bubbling up in your thoughts while reading this book, or maybe there's some new issue that just popped up for you today. The worksheet can help with any dilemma, but it's specifically been created with parenting dilemmas in mind.

While we all have things we're working through and struggling with, it can be difficult for some to identify issues that require a value-based approach. If you need to, take a look back at chapter 3 and pick something that you feel inwardly or outwardly conflicted about. Any type of conflict can provide an opportunity to take a look at your values and recalibrate your approach.

An important thing to consider when identifying your dilemma is "What choice, decision, or action is at stake?" Some dilemmas have clear-cut decisions or actions tied to them; for example, "What school is right for my son?" or "My child's school contacted me to tell me that my son has been skipping class; how do I confront him about it?"

Many dilemmas, especially ones involving internal conflict, aren't obvious choices between courses of action.

The other morning I was on a walk with a dear friend who's very psychologically aware, insightful, and self-reflective. As we so often do, we regaled one another with our latest dilemmas, what our psyches have been "chewing on" over the past several weeks—our work, our families, and our kids. My friend noted her disappointment in her twelve-year-old son's recent lack of interest in playing music. In his downtime, rather than reaching for his guitar, he reached for his phone. And rather than sitting at the piano, he lay on his bed, passively scrolling, connecting to a computerized reality and disconnecting from the live people around him.

As a musician herself, it "killed her" to see him depriving himself of the joy that he had always gleaned from music, not to mention his innate gifts. She understands the way that music moves her and reaches her soul. She worried that his lack of initiative, resistance to practicing, and the time spent on TikTok and social media were consuming his time, and depriving his soul. "Seeing him on his bed, phone in hand, laughing at who-knows-what—it depresses me," she said.

While she was certainly facing a dilemma, it wasn't immediately clear what courses of action were available. All that was clear was that she had a dilemma and she wasn't sure how to proceed.

If you find yourself in a similar boat, don't worry. As far as Step 1 is concerned, all you need to do is write down your dilemma. As we progress further through the conversation (and down the worksheet), courses of action will present themselves. We won't worry about coming up with potential plans of action until Step 4, anyway.

STEP 2: Define your values

Actually identifying what your values are seems simple: Just pick out your top ten values from the provided list (see List of Values below). However, I recommend taking your time as you go through this step. It's worth digging deeper to make sure that we are being accurate about what our values are. We get so used to being our "social" and/ or "achievement-oriented" selves that we may find ourselves choosing values because it's what we think we *should* value, rather than what we actually value. This is just another way of falling into the behavioral trap of making decisions based on anxiety. If we're making decisions based on what we think our values *should* be, rather than what they are, we're likely to remain stuck in internal or external conflicts.

As you reflect on what your values might be, walk yourself through one (or more) of the following exercises:

- Make a list of all the things you've done over the past few days and identify moments when you felt the best—when you felt particularly content or alive.
- What was it about those moments that made you feel that way? What were you doing? How were you behaving? Which of the values reflect those qualities?
- Reflect on what your perfect day might look like.

LIST OF VALUES

Achievement-oriented	Autonomous	Confident	Considered excellent	Non-conforming	Resilient
Adaptable	Being challenged	Being in control	Faithful	Obedient	Resourceful
Ambitious	Compassionate	Cooperative	Family-oriented	Optimistic	Responsible
Assertive	Competitive	Courageous	Fearless	Passionate	Self-disciplined
Attractive	Someone who fits in	Creative	Secure	Peaceful	Selfless
Financially secure	Generous	Curious	Knowledgeable	Having pleasure	Sensual
Forgiving	Gracious	Being independent	Leader	Powerful	Spiritual
Having friends	Healthy	Being internally harmonious	Having leisure time	Precise	Stable
Frugal	Helpful to others	Having integrity	Loyal	Rational	Successful
Being or having fun	Honest	Having intellectual status	Moderate	Recognized	Trustworthy
Wise	Humble	Being fair-minded	Wealthy	Reliable	Having variety

- What would you be doing? How would you be behaving? Which of the values reflect those qualities?
- If you were to write a personal or family mission statement, which of the words provided would you be inclined to include?
- What do you admire about your role models?
- Which of the values reflect their qualities?
- The most painful moments of our life can also be indicators. Remember moments of great discomfort or emotional pain. It's likely that in those moments the things you value most were *not* present.

- Example: If we feel a great amount of pain when we discover we've been lied to, then "being honest" is likely something we value.

"I know what's important to me," my friend said, as we stood admiring a blossoming tree (which she even knew the name of). "Until now, I have been so clear about what I want for my son—to commit to an interest. I want him to persevere through challenges, make progress in his field, experience joy in doing it, and be motivated to invest himself in it."

On the surface, my friend's values, when considering her upset around her son not playing music as much anymore, could be interpreted as "being creative" or "being playful." As a very self-aware person, she was able to identify the heart of her issue. What she really valued was commitment and self-discipline. Her concern wasn't simply that he wasn't playing music, but that he wasn't going to reap the benefits that come with long-term commitment.

STEP 3: Indulge your anxiety. What are your biggest worries about the dilemma?

Pull out your anxious thoughts and see if you can identify any cognitive distortions that might be at play. We can be thrown off course when deciding what actions to take if our perceptions don't align with reality. Deliberately letting our anxiety out of the bottle helps us pull out our thoughts and examine them more objectively.

My friend's anxiety was simple.

"I cannot believe these words are coming out of my mouth," she complained, "especially with you, the achievement anxiety expert! But he's approaching high school, and then, college! This is not good. If he can't commit to something I know he loves, like playing music, how will he be able to handle studying or homework?"

She was stuck in a classic case of catastrophizing: "Because my son isn't focusing on his music, that means he won't be able to focus in school and will struggle academically." Before I was able to step in and ask some questions to challenge this line of thinking, we were interrupted by a call from her husband. Her husband and son were out of state for a baseball tournament. Apparently, her son was playing on a field that he had dreamt of playing on for his entire life. As the starting pitcher for his team, he had demonstrated passion for the sport and dedicated hours to practice, rain or shine; whether he was tired or not, he was determined to improve. He was an involved team member and leader, and had recently become the star pitcher for the team.

Her call with her husband had done a better job of challenging her anxious thoughts than I ever could have done. It reminded her that her son was, in fact, very committed to the things he was passionate about. His passion just so happened to be baseball, and maybe not music after all.

"Although," she admitted sheepishly, "he still takes weekly guitar lessons. For a twelve-year-old," she wondered aloud, "that may be enough."

STEP 4: Use your values to find a creative solution to your parenting dilemma

Now that you've aired your anxious thoughts, you'll have more space to use the creative and rational parts of your brain to make a decision. Use the values you listed in Step 2 to generate ideas for what you can do next that will be aligned with your values. Try to avoid coming up with the perfect solution. In all likelihood, it doesn't exist. Instead, imagine a number of ways that your values could come into play.

The solution for my friend presented itself readily: "If I value commitment," she said, "then the solution is to support what he's already committed to—baseball."

But let's say that she hadn't gotten that perfectly timed call from her husband, reminding her about her son's commitment to baseball. She could have also come up with the following:

- "If I value commitment, then a possible solution might be to have a conversation with him about his music, to try and discover why he's lost/losing interest in it."
- "If I value commitment, then a possible solution might be to ask him if there is anything else he wants to commit his time and energy to."

STEP 5: Make an imperfect decision or take imperfect action

No decision you make or action you take will lead to a perfect resolution of your dilemma. The desire for perfection is a product of both our achievement-centered culture and our anxiety. So when you feel the desire to be perfect arise, say "Thank you very much, but I've decided to be imperfect today." We can be as self-aware as possible, avoid reacting to our anxieties, make decisions, and perform actions that align with our values. We are living, breathing, adaptable beings, and we can always readjust/change course down the road if need be.

Because my friend was a musician herself, she had an attachment to her son playing music. She wanted him to love it as much as she did—and she recognized that the imperfect solution to her dilemma was to support his commitment to baseball. In that solution, he got to display the character traits that she valued and she got to be a supportive and proud parent.

As she reached this conclusion, she pointed to and named another tree on the verge of blossoming. The branches that had been dormant and bare all winter were covered in blooming buds. The buds on each branch were flowering at different rates. Many of the buds had reached their full potential while others were still "waiting" to open. They couldn't be forced, and every bud was not going to bloom this season. Yet, in its entirety, the tree was beautiful and flourishing. A poignant reminder that allowing things to be "good enough" is always a healthy choice.

Wait; do I have to take action and make decisions that align with my values all the time?

Those of us who try to be perfect (even if we know better) fall easily into a new trap once we know that values-based decision-making is possible. "Now I have to do this all the time!" we may think. "How do I do it perfectly?"

I still fall into those thought patterns even though I've been practicing being imperfect for decades now. The short answer is that this is not possible. However, there are a couple of additional things we can practice to align ourselves with our values more often:

1) Watching what we talk about or emphasize

A common idea I hear parents express is that they value "grit" (aka, strength of character) over achievement outcomes. While this may be theoretical, the way parents talk to their kids often doesn't align with this value. When their teen arrives home from a soccer match, the first question a parent might ask is "Did you win?" or "What was the score?" These questions convey a concern with the outcome of the game—they are about their teens' "achievement metrics" and not about the teens' experience.

Since grit is the core value here, the parent could change their questions to reflect this instead: "Was there a difference in how you played this time? Any areas of progress?" or "How well did you play as a team?" The parent can also intentionally reflect or positively reinforce the attributes, traits, and qualities that they value the most: "I could tell you were getting tired on the field, but it looked like you were determined to try your best until the whistle blew!"

2) Creating an environment that reinforces our values

A parent who values faith in God may regularly attend religious services, make sure that there are readily accessible religious readings in the home, and invoke faith in daily discussions. They can make it easy and accessible for their kids to participate in faith-based activities.

A parent who values physical health might spend time meal planning with their kid, making sure healthy snacks are readily accessible, and working with their teen to come up with ideas for well-balanced meals at home their teen enjoys.

3) Setting goals that align with our values

When we set a goal, it is likely to reflect a quality that is meaningful or important to us. If a parent forgoes certain material luxuries to reach the goal of saving a certain amount of money in a college fund, this may be reflective of the value of education.

What happens when my values conflict?

As we engage in this complex and not-so-straightforward process of aligning our behavior with our values, one of the many challenges we are likely to encounter is that values are strongly influenced by particular moments in time, stages of development, or life crises (positive or negative). Essentially, our values do not hold the same weight or meaning for us all of the time.

All the values we hold coexist but shift in degree of importance depending upon the situation. When I'm on vacation I value freedom and self-expression above all. When I'm on the subway I value peace and personal space. My valuing self-expression is in direct conflict with my valuing peace and personal space when I get on the subway and a crew of dancers decides to practice their latest moves practically on top of me. This sense of valuing two things simultaneously that seem incompatible with one another is often especially evident when we're anxious or our thinking becomes more binary.

In such cases, we require more creativity and clarity of thought to reconcile our actions and our values. Being confronted by dancing on the subway is a small matter, but what happens in situations that feel more dire? In chapter 7, Chris the Avoider, the father valued non-competitiveness but also agency. Part of his dilemma was, if he allowed his son to do what he wanted (agency), then his son would engage more in competitive sports and the corresponding culture.

I always encourage parents to consider expressions of value in accordance with the developmental stage and temperament of the child in question. In this case, a satisfactory compromise was reached, but it required the parent to do some deep digging into what he really valued and what he wanted for his son.

Ideally, we experience a sense of continuity and reliability with our values. However, each situation and moment in time is unique, and we need to allow for that. It's important to remember that the final step in a values-driven approach is always to "Make an imperfect decision."

Conclusion

It is often said that authors write the book they need to read and that teachers teach what they need to learn. I am no exception.

Twenty years ago, I wrote my doctoral dissertation on the impact of working motherhood on a daughter's sense of self, while my daughter was in utero. Fittingly, I began writing this book the year she began high school. This was either a parenting midlife crisis or, more likely, my way of managing my own parental achievement anxiety as a newly minted parent of a high-schooler.

Yet my intention to dig deeply into this topic had not been solely based on my personal efforts for preparedness. Instead, it had been largely prompted by my grave concern for the growing number of adolescents in my practice (and their parents) who were manifesting achievement stress. So, with a passion for psychological theory, my evolving ideas on the issue, and a long-held desire to write a book, I set out on this personal and professional challenge.

As so often happens, my research and my writing process led me to unexpected insights and understandings of the issues. I found that the themes which emerged on the topic paralleled my writing experience. For the past seven years, I have faced the dilemmas and learned the lessons that I teach in this book, over and over again, from the macro to the micro. My hope is that by reading this book, you, too, have been either introduced to or reminded of several important messages. I hope that your perspectives have widened, your self-awareness has deepened, and that you've learned some new skills to take with you as you continue your parenting journey.

As I reflect on the many lessons I've learned, I'll leave you with five highlights to bear in mind long after you've closed this book:

1) Remember the importance of process over outcome.

While my expressed goal was to complete the book, my writing process has been the more unexpectedly invaluable (and humbling) experience. Through many rejections, failures, frustrations, and feelings of inadequacy, I was forced to bounce back more times than I can count, and it was in the process of doing so that I learned, grew, and evolved. I am certain that my own children and my patients will benefit from the critical experience and skills that I've gained through this enormous challenge. While the achievement of completing a book has been rewarding, the more valuable lessons were gleaned from the process of my getting there.

As you navigate the rocky terrain of parenting adolescents, remember to trust and value your teens' process and the messages you impart while doing so. Teens have endless opportunities to develop essential emotional skills, tolerate their frustrations, endure disappointments, and challenge themselves throughout this life stage. When we focus exclusively on their acceptance into a dream college, we lose sight of the important life lessons which invariably occur during their development. Our focus on the process, rather than the outcome, conveys how much you value them—now!

2) Assume the growth mind-set, for your teens and for yourself.

Despite your being the adult in the relationship, you are also an evolving human being. Like your teen, you still have the capacity to grow, expand, and shift perspectives, particularly on your multi-decade parenting ride. It's never too late to shift course, reconsider a plan, or update your narrative. I have often fantasized about having T-shirts printed that say "Still Under Construction." Though you may fear that your current decisions are irreversible or permanent, many can be modified along the way. Human development is not linear; it ebbs and flows. We progress and regress—that's how growth happens.

3) Reconciling values and decisions is often a challenge.

Publishing a book, like parenting a human, is not as pure a process as I had imagined. Before doing either, I had heard that it would difficult and challenging, but the aspects that stuck in my craw were not the ones

I had expected. Like parenting, the book publishing world has changed significantly over the years. It involves marketing, branding, appealing to the powers that be, and engaging on social media. As a psychotherapist whose career is based on confidentiality, privacy, and safety, this was more than I'd bargained for. Unwilling to compromise my values, the realities of navigating the unfamiliar publishing landscape have tested my previously unquestioned idealism.

Likewise, as you navigate the realities of this generation's hyper-achievement landscape, your ideals and values will be put to new tests. I encourage you to maintain your values as your North Star, so that you can devise creative and values-aligned solutions to your parenting dilemmas.

4) Allow your child's developmental phase to inhabit center stage.

While you view yourself as a guide, you are not the leader or director of your teen's trajectory. Meet your child where they are and view them within this context as you walk alongside them. Remember that your teen's essential tasks during this phase of life are to explore their identity and separate from their parents. This is as biologically essential as their physical growth. As you communicate with them, maintain this awareness.

5) Remember that we are wired for protection.

In the spirit of self-compassion and self-awareness, we are all just trying to live more comfortably in our own skin. Despite anxiety's bad reputation, it is essential for our survival—part of our protective wiring. When you find yourself becoming anxious, try not to judge, criticize, or repress it. Anxiety, like all our emotions, is a window into our needs. Our emotions originate from our deep ancestral human need to protect ourselves and protect our young from harm, emotional and physical. Knowing ourselves allows us to help our teens know themselves, and enables us to know them, in the most human and authentically successful way. Ultimately, this is what we are all seeking, teens and parents alike.

Appendix

The Parenting Decision-Making Worksheet

"For when you're torn between what you should do, and what you want to do for your teen."

Created by Dr. Dana Dorfman

www.drdanadorfman.com

As parents, we're constantly making decisions, big and small, that will affect our teen's success in life, such as:

- What school should they go to?
- How much time should they spend on homework?
- How many after-school activities should they be involved in?

It's an incredible privilege to make these kinds of choices, and it can be extremely stressful. We can end up feeling torn between what we feel we should do, and what we want to do. To manage the anxiety, we might make pros and cons lists, ask friends for opinions, surf parenting blogs for expert advice, or even fight with our spouse, partner, or teen.

What we actually need to be doing is making decisions based on our values. I created this worksheet to help you do just that. This is not meant to be a quick-fix solution—I don't believe in those—but rather a tool to help you start imagining creative solutions for what can feel like intractable paradoxes.

1. What is the parenting dilemma or parenting decision that you're dealing with or feeling challenged by right now?

2. Define your family's values.

We can't make values-based decisions unless we know what our values are. Lists of values usually include qualities like honesty, responsibility, creativity, and success, but you can also include more specific descriptions of what you value, like having a five-year plan, volunteering in your community, and weekly family dinners. Here's a list of values (qualities or ways of being) to help you get started:

Being achievement-oriented
Being adaptable
Being ambitious
Being assertive
Being attractive
Being autonomous
Being challenged
Being compassionate
Being competitive
Being someone who fits in
Being confident
Being in control
Being cooperative
Being courageous
Being creative
Being curious
Being considered excellent
Being faithful
Being family-oriented
Being fearless
Being secure
Being financially secure
Being forgiving

Having friends
Being frugal
Being or having fun
Being generous
Being gracious
Being healthy
Being helpful to others
Being honest
Being humble
Being independent
Being internally harmonious
Having integrity
Having intellectual status
Being fair-minded
Being knowledgeable
Being a leader
Having leisure time
Being loyal
Being moderate
Being nonconforming
Being obedient
Being optimistic
Being passionate
Being peaceful
Having pleasure
Being powerful
Being precise
Being rational
Being recognized
Being reliable
Being resilient
Being resourceful
Being responsible
Being self-disciplined
Being selfless
Being sensual
Being spiritual
Being stable

Being successful
Being trustworthy
Having variety
Being wealthy
Being wise

3. Make a list of five to ten things—activities, qualities, or ways of behaving—that you value right now. (You can use the list of values above for inspiration, if you'd like.) If you have a spouse, or partner, I recommend that they make their own list.

4. From these list(s), circle the three to five values you want your family to live by. Write a sentence for each that demonstrates how you'd put these values into action, using the following example:

Since I value _____, I will (or continue to) _____.

5. Indulge your anxiety. What are your biggest worries about the dilemma? What are some of your anxious thoughts?

When anxiety drives our decisions, we think in extremes. In this step, we're going to allow your anxiety to take center stage. Write down any thoughts that come to mind, no matter how ludicrous they may sound! Here are some anxious-thought prompts:

- *Catastrophize:* What is the worst outcome you can imagine?
- *Black-and-white thinking:* What are the most extreme outcomes—the worst-case scenario and the best?
- *Labeling:* What's the story that you're telling yourself about this scenario? What words are you using to describe the situation, the emotions surrounding it, and people involved?

6. Use your values to find a creative solution to your parenting dilemma.

Now that your anxiety feels like it has been seen and heard, you'll have more space to use the creative and rational parts of your brain to make a decision. You're going to use the values you listed in Step 2 to generate ideas that are aligned with your values. Fill in the blanks for each of your family's values, following this example:

If I/we value _____, a solution could be to_____.

7. Make an imperfect decision.

Knowing that no decision will result in perfection, and that it's always possible to pivot and change course if I/we find I'm/we're going in the wrong direction, a solution to this dilemma that aligns with my/our values is to:

Answering the questions in this worksheet won't produce a quick fix or a perfect solution, but having this conversation will create space for you to see beyond your parenting dilemma, so that you can make a decision that is driven by your values, not your anxiety.

If you have any questions, or would like to share your experience using this process, please join our Parenting Paradox Facebook Group, or email me at dana@drdanadorfman.com.

Notes

CHAPTER 1

1. "The Social Dilemma: Social Media and Your Mental Health," McLean Hospital, January 21, 2022, www.mcleanhospital.org/essential/it-or-not-social -medias-affecting-your-mental-health.

2. "Declaration of a National Emergency in Child and Adolescent Mental Health," American Academy of Pediatrics, October 19, 2021, www.aap.org/ en/advocacy/child-and-adolescent-healthy-mental-development/aap-aacap-cha -declaration-of-a-national-emergency-in-child-and-adolescent-mental-health/.

3. "Declaration of a National Emergency in Child and Adolescent Mental Health," American Academy of Pediatrics, October 19, 2021, www.aap.org/ en/advocacy/child-and-adolescent-healthy-mental-development/aap-aacap-cha -declaration-of-a-national-emergency-in-child-and-adolescent-mental-health/.

4. Richard Schiffman, "Climate Anxiety Is Widespread among Youth: Can They Overcome It?" *National Geographic*, June 29, 2022.

5. Jean Twenge, *IGen: Why Today's Super-Connected Kids Are Growing Up Less Rebellious, More Tolerant, Less-Happy—and Completely Unprepared for Adulthood* (New York: Atria, 2017).

6. Michelle Goldberg, "The Mental Health Toll of Trump-Era Politics," *New York Times*, January 21, 2022.

7. Anna Sutherland, "Why Parenting Has Gotten More Difficult," Institute for Family Studies, February 19, 2019, https://ifstudies.org/blog/why-parenting -has-gotten-more-difficult/.

8. William Deresiewicz, *Excellent Sheep: The Miseducation of the American Elite and the Way to a Meaningful Life* (New York: Free Press, 2015), 32.

189

9. Frank Bruni, *Where You Go Is Not Who You'll Be: An Antidote to the College Admissions Mania* (New York: Grand Central Publishing, 2015).

10. "JED's POV on Student Mental Health and Well-Being in Fall Campus Reopening," The Jed Foundation, August 30, 2021.

11. Debra Cano Ramos, "Suicide Prevention Program Increases Awareness," *Inside*, California State University, Fullerton, July 22, 2008.

12. "The Children We Mean to Raise: The Real Messages Adults Are Sending about Values," *Making Caring Common*, Harvard Graduate School of Education, December 13, 2021.

13. Jennifer Breheny Wallace, "Perspective: Students in High-Achieving Schools Are Now Named an 'At-Risk' Group, Study Says," *Washington Post*, October 24, 2019.

14. Beth Cooper Benjamin, "Trend Lines: Challenging Achievement Culture in Schools," National Association of Independent Schools (NAIS), www.nais.org/magazine/independent-school/winter-2022/trend-lines-challenging-achievement-culture-in-schools/, accessed April 5, 2022.

15. Suniya S. Luthar and Chris C. Sexton, "The High Price of Affluence," *Advances in Child Development and Behavior*, vol. 32 (2004), 125–62.

16. Luthar and Sexton, "The High Price of Affluence," 125–62.

17. Tim Kautz, James Heckman, Ron Diris, Bas ter Weel, and Lex Borghans, "Fostering and Measuring Skills: Improving Cognitive and Non-Cognitive Skills to Promote Lifetime Success," *NBER Working Paper No. 20749,* April 2015, 2–124.

18. Laura Chapman, Rosie Hutson, Abby Dunn, Maddy Brown, Ella Savill, Sam Cartwright-Hatton, "The Impact of Treating Parental Anxiety on Children's Mental Health: An Empty Systematic Review," *Journal of Anxiety Disorders*, vol. 88 (May 2022).

CHAPTER 2

1. William Shakespeare, *Hamlet* (New York: American Scholar Publications, 1965).

2. "Sugar: The Bitter Truth," *YouTube*, www.youtube.com/watch?v=dBnniua6-oM.

CHAPTER 3

1. "Psychology Tools | Evidence-Based CBT Worksheets," *Psychology Tools*, 2018, https://www.psychologytools.com/.

2. Courtney Ackerman, "Cognitive Distortions: When Your Brain Lies to You (+ PDF Worksheets)," PositivePsychology.com, September 29, 2017.

3. Leo Tolstoy, *Anna Karenina* (Moscow, ID: Canon Press, 2020).

4. American Psychological Association (APA), "APA Dictionary of Psychology," Apa.org, 2014, https://dictionary.apa.org/.

5. The Beck Institute, "Cognitive Restructuring in CBT," Beck Institute, June 8, 2021.

6. APA, "APA Dictionary of Psychology."

7. The Beck Institute, "Cognitive Restructuring in CBT."

8. APA, "APA Dictionary of Psychology."

9. The Beck Institute, "Cognitive Restructuring in CBT."

10. APA, "APA Dictionary of Psychology."

11. "Psychology Tools | Evidence-Based CBT Worksheets."

12. APA, "APA Dictionary of Psychology."

13. APA, "APA Dictionary of Psychology."

14. "Psychology Tools | Evidence-Based CBT Worksheets."

15. "Psychology Tools | Evidence-Based CBT Worksheets."

16. "Psychology Tools | Evidence-Based CBT Worksheets."

17. Additional recommended readings on anxiety: Judson Brewer, *Unwinding Anxiety: New Science Shows How to Break the Cycles of Worry and Fear to Heal Your Mind* (New York: Avery, Penguin Random House LLC, 2021); Wendy Suzuki and Billie Fitzpatrick, *Good Anxiety: Harnessing the Power of the Most Misunderstood Emotion* (New York: Atria Books, 2021). Additional recommended readings on generalized anxiety disorder assessment: Robert L. Spitzer, Kurt Kroenke, Janet B. W. Williams, and Bernd Löwe, "A Brief Measure for Assessing Generalized Anxiety Disorder," *Archives of Internal Medicine* 166 (10) (2006): 1092. https://doi.org/10.1001/archinte.166.10.1092.

CHAPTER 12

1. Carol Graham and Michael E. O'Hanlon, "Harvard Said 'No'? Be Happy!" *Brookings*, May 20, 2014; Danielle Wiener-Bronner, "That Ivy League Degree Won't Make You Happy in the Real World," *The Atlantic*, May 6, 2014.

2. Madeline Levine, PhD, *Teach Your Children Well: Why Values and Coping Skills Matter More than Grades, Trophies, or "Fat Envelopes"* (London: Harper Perennial, 2016), 248.

3. Levine, *Teach Your Children Well.*

4. David Brooks, *The Road to Character* (New York: Random House, 2016).

5. Donald W. Winnicott, "Ego Distortion in Terms of True and False Self (1960)," in *The Maturational Processes and the Facilitating Environment: Studies in the Theory of Emotional Development* (1st ed.) (London: Routledge, 1984).

Bibliography

Abeles, Vicki, Grace Rubenstein, and Lynda Weinman. *Beyond Measure: Rescuing an Overscheduled, Overtested, Underestimated Generation*. New York: Simon & Schuster Paperbacks, 2016.

Aburdene Derhally, Lena. "About That Parental Anxiety . . . " *Washington Post*, April 3, 2015. www.washingtonpost.com/news/parenting/wp/2015/04/03/about-that-parental-anxiety/.

Anderegg, David. *Worried All the Time: Rediscovering the Joy in Parenthood in an Age of Anxiety*. New York: Free Press, 2004.

Baum, Sandy, and Stella Flores. "Higher Education and Children in Immigrant Families Higher Education and Children in Immigrant Families," vol. 21, no. 1 (Spring 2011). www.futureofchildren.org, https://files.eric.ed.gov/fulltext/EJ920372.pdf.

Beck, Aaron T. 1963. "Thinking and Depression." *Archives of General Psychiatry* 9 (4) (1963): 324. https://doi.org/10.1001/archpsyc.1963.01720160014002.

Beck, Judith S. *Cognitive Behavior Therapy: Basics and Beyond*, 2nd ed. New York: Guilford Press, 2011.

Begley, Sharon. "A Special Feature from *Newsweek*: The Parent Trap," 1998. Washingtonpost.com. www.washingtonpost.com/wp-srv/newsweek/parent090798a.htm.

Borglass, Steve. "Worried about Anxiety? Don't Be; It's Good for You." *Forbes*, January 25, 2013. www.forbes.com/sites/stevenberglas/2013/01/25/worried-about-anxiety-dont-be-its-often-good-for-you/?sh=38d0941a63fb.

Brewer, Judson. *Unwinding Anxiety: New Science Shows How to Break the Cycles of Worry and Fear to Heal Your Mind*. New York: Avery, Penguin Random House, 2021.

Brooks, David. *The Road to Character*. New York: Random House, 2016.

Bruni, Frank. *Where You Go Is Not Who You'll Be: An Antidote to the College Admissions Mania*. New York: Grand Central Publishing, 2016.

Carter, Christine. *The New Adolescence: Raising Happy and Successful Teens in an Age of Anxiety and Distraction.* Dallas, TX: BenBella Books, 2020.

Cassani Davis, Laura. "The Ivy League, Mental Illness, and the Meaning of Life." *The Atlantic*, August 19, 2014.

Center for Parenting Education, The. "Using Your Values to Raise Your Children." The Center for Parenting Education, n.d. Accessed April 19, 2022. https://centerforparentingeducation.org/library-of-articles/indulgence-values /values-matter-using-your-values-to-raise-caring-responsible-resilient -children-what-are-values/#:~:text=Values%20are%20very%20important %20in.

Challenge Success. "A Fit over Rankings: Why College Engagement Matters More than Selectivity," May 14, 2021. https://www.google.com/search ?q=challenge+success+a+fit+over+rankings&oq=challenge+success+&aqs =chrome.1.69i57j0i20i263i512j0i51218.5340j0j7&sourceid=chrome&ie =UTF-8.

Clark, Denise, Maureen Brown, and Sarah Miles. 2015. *Overloaded and Underprepared: Strategies for Stronger Schools and Healthy, Successful Kids.* San Francisco: Jossey-Bass, A Wiley Brand, 2015.

"Cognitive Behavior Therapy," n.d. *Psychology Tools.* Accessed April 19, 2022. www.psychologytools.com/what.

Condensed Lectures, and Robert Lustig, MD. "Sugar: The Bitter Truth— Condensed Lectures," 2016. *YouTube.* https://www.youtube.com/watch?v =T8G8tLsl_A4.

Damour, Lisa. *Untangled: Guiding Teenage Girls through the Seven Transitions into Adulthood.* London: Atlantic Books, 2017.

———. *Under Pressure: Confronting the Epidemic of Stress and Anxiety in Girls.* New York: Ballantine Books, 2020.

Deresiewicz, William. *Excellent Sheep: The Miseducation of the American Elite and the Way to a Meaningful Life.* New York: Free Press, 2015.

Divecha, Diana. "Our Teens Are More Stressed than Ever: Why, and What Can You Do about It?" *Developmental Science.* May 9, 2019. www .developmentalscience.com/blog/2019/5/7/our-teens-are-more-stressed-than -ever.

Doepke, Matthias, and Fabrizio Zilibotti.

Elliott, Christine, and William Reynolds III. "Making It Millennial." Theatlantic.com. 2015. www.theatlantic.com/sponsored/deloitte-shifts/ making-it-millennial/259/.

EV Scarlett. "Character Core Values Archives." *The Character Comma.* May 8, 2016. https://thecharactercomma.com/tag/character-core-values/.

Fraiberg, Selma, Edna Adelson, and Vivian Shapiro. "Ghosts in the Nursery." *Journal of the American Academy of Child Psychiatry* 14 (3) (1975): 387– 421. https://doi.org/10.1016/s0002-7138(09)61442-4.

Frankl, Viktor E. *Man's Search for Meaning*. Boston: Beacon Press, (1946) 2006.

Gregory, Sean. "How Kid Sports Turned Pro." *Time Magazine*, September 4, 2017. https://time.com/magazine/us/4913681/september-4th-2017-vol-190 -no-9-u-s/.

Grolnick, Wendy S., and Kathy Seal. *Pressured Parents, Stressed-out Kids: Dealing with Competition While Raising a Successful Child*. Amherst, NY: Prometheus Books, 2008.

Gross, Terry. "College Students and Their Parents Face a Campus Mental Health Epidemic." Radio Show, 2019. National Public Radio.

Guessoum, Sélim Benjamin, Jonathan Lachal, Rahmeth Radjack, Emilie Carretier, Sevan Minassian, Laelia Benoit, and Marie Rose Moro. "Adolescent Psychiatric Disorders during the COVID-19 Pandemic and Lockdown." *Psychiatry Research* 291 (September 2020): 113264. https://doi.org/10.1016 /j.psychres.2020.113264.

Hayes, Steven. "10 Signs You Know What Matters." *Psychology Today*, September 2018. www.psychologytoday.com/us/articles/201809/10-signs -you-know-what-matters.

Kindlon, Daniel J. *Too Much of a Good Thing: Raising Children of Character in an Indulgent Age*. New York: Miramax Books, 2002.

Kohli, Sonali. "Study: Kids Who Grow up with Anxious Parents Take on Their Anxiety." *Quartz*. May 12, 2015. https://qz.com/403299/study-kids-who -grow-up-with-anxious-parents-take-on-their-anxiety/.

Levine, Madeline. *The Price of Privilege: How the Culture of Affluence Challenges Parents and Puts Children at Risk*. New York: HarperCollins, 2006.

———. *Teach Your Children Well: Why Values and Coping Skills Matter More than Grades, Trophies, or "Fat Envelopes."* London: Harper Perennial, 2016.

———. "Kids Don't Need to Stay 'On Track' to Succeed." *The Atlantic*. February 16, 2020. www.theatlantic.com/family/archive/2020/02/path -success-squiggly-line/606631/.

———. *Ready or Not: Preparing Our Kids to Thrive in an Uncertain World*. New York: Harper Perennial, 2021.

Lythcott-Haims, Julie. *How to Raise an Adult*. New York: St. Martin's Griffin, 2016.

Mogel, Wendy. *The Blessing of a B Minus: Using Jewish Teachings to Raise Resilient Teenagers*. New York: Scribner, 2011.

Morse, Robert, Eric Brooks, and Matt Mason. "How *U.S. News* Calculated the 2020 Best Colleges Rankings." *US News & World Report*. 2020. www .usnews.com/education/best-colleges/articles/how-us-news-calculated-the -rankings.

Pink, Daniel H. *Drive: The Surprising Truth about What Motivates Us*. Edinburgh, Scotland: Canongate Books Ltd., (2009) 2018.

Pope, Denise Clark. *Doing School: How We Are Creating a Generation of Stressed-Out, Materialistic, and Miseducated Students*. Paw Prints, 2008.

Seemiller, Corey, and Meghan Grace. *Generation Z Goes to College.* John Wiley & Sons, 2016.

Smith, Emily Esfahani. "Opinion: Teenagers Are Struggling, and It's Not Just Lockdown." *New York Times*, May 4, 2021, sec. Opinion. www.nytimes.com /2021/05/04/opinion/coronavirus-mental-health-teenagers.html.

Spencer, Kyle. "It Takes a Suburb: A Town Struggles to Ease Student Stress." *New York Times*, April 5, 2017, sec. Education. https://www.nytimes.com /2017/04/05/education/edlife/overachievers-student-stress-in-high-school -.html.

Steinberg, Laurence. *Age of Opportunity: Lessons from the New Science of Adolescence*. Boston: Mariner Books, Houghton Mifflin Harcourt, 2015.

Steinmetz, Katy. "Help! My Parents Are Millennials." *Time*, October 26, 2015. https://time.com/magazine/us/4074544/october-26th-2015-vol-186-no-17-u -s/.

Suzuki, Wendy, and Billie Fitzpatrick. *Good Anxiety: Harnessing the Power of the Most Misunderstood Emotion*. New York: Atria Books, 2021.

Torrez, Eileen. "Dilemmas Archives." *Parenting.* June 15, 2014. http:// greatschools.org/gk/category/dilemmas/.

Tough, Paul. *How Children Succeed: Confidence, Curiosity and the Hidden Power of Character*. London: Arrow Books, 2014.

Twenge, Jean M. *iGen: Why Today's Super-Connected Kids Are Growing Up Less Rebellious, More Tolerant, Less Happy—and Completely Unprepared for Adulthood (and What This Means for the Rest of Us)*. New York: Atria Paperback, 2018.

Wallace, Kelly. "Narcissistic Parenting: When You Compete through Your Child." CNN. July 24, 2015. www.cnn.com/2015/07/24/health/health -narcissistic-parenting-children-impact/index.html.

Warner, Judith. *Perfect Madness: Motherhood in the Age of Anxiety*. New York: Riverhead Books, 2006.

Weissbourd, Rick. *The Parents We Mean to Be: How Well-Intentioned Adults Undermine Children's Moral and Emotional Development*. Boston: Houghton Mifflin Harcourt, 2010.

YouTube. "Race to Nowhere," 2015. *YouTube.* www.youtube.com/watch?v =BE7TLXbXROg.

Index

academic success, 14
achievement anxiety, 3
achievement fanatic, 1
achievement-oriented values, *172*
achievement stress, 179
ACT test, 95–96, 100–101
addiction, to sugar, 19
affluence, 15
agency: Clairvoyants related to, 123–24, 127; GSC and, 86; Sculptor parents with, 70–72; Shepherds related to, 133–34, 137–39, 142
Alice. *See* Crowd-Pleasers
American Psychological Association (APA), 37–38
anxiety, 1–4. *See also specific topics*
anxiety as new sugar: addiction related to, 19; anxiety shaming in, 20–22; anxiety's sweet spot in, 21–22; brain in, 26, 27–28; collaboration in, 26–27; college essay and, 24–26; conflict related to, 25–26; overwhelm and, 25, 26, 27; parenting anxiety in, 27–28; parenting outlet in, 23; predictions in, 26–27; quantity of, 24–26;

simple solution for, 28–29; sugar quantity in, 24–26; values in, 27; weight-loss related to, 19
anxiety management, 27, 28, 34–35; of GSC, 83–84; in parenting achievement anxiety, 17; for Shepherds, 140–41; for survival, 181; techniques for, 183
anxiety patterns, 28–29
anxiety shaming, 20–22
anxiety spirals, 13, 49; of Avoider, 111–13; of Clairvoyants, 121–22; of Correctors, 150–51; of Crowd-Pleasers, 97–98; of GSC, 84; of Replicators, 163; Sculptor parents related to, 64–66; for Shepherds, 139; in worry works, 33–34
APA. *See* American Psychological Association
apathy, 56–57, 61–65
archetypes, 4
athleticism, 107–9
autonomous values, *172*
avoidance, 25–26
Avoiders, 51, 177; achievement culture and, 107; anxiety dealing

197

anxiety game of, 84–86; anxiety management of, 83–84; anxiety overcome for, 88–89; anxiety spiral of, 84; black-and-white thinking of, 82, 87–88; breaking the cycle for, 87–88; breathwork for, 81; communication for, 87; creative problem-solving of, 85; decision making in, 77–80, 82–84; decisiveness of, 80–81; desperation of, 79; dilemma for, 79–80; door #2 for, 77–79, 87; doubts related to, 77, 83; focus of, 86; goal achievement for, 77; immigration related to, 81–82, 86–87; indecision validity of, 81, 84, 85, 89; *Let's Make a Deal* related to, 76; magnification by, 88; new motherhood of, 75; not-knowing related to, 84; panic attack of, 75, 83; perks for, 77; pitfalls related to, 85–86; private or public school for, 78–80; protection from, 85; rationalism of, 77; thought distortions of, 87–88; trauma of, 80–82; uncertainty related to, 77, 78–79; values of, 86; working-motherhood plan for, 75–76; worst-case scenario of, 88–89
"game the system," 14–15
Generation X, 13
global pandemic mental health, 9
goal achievement, 77
goals: for Sculptor parents, 69; values of values related to, 177
"good enough," 175
grit, 176
growth mind-set, 180
GSC. *See* Game Show Contestant

happiness, 95, 167–68

harnessing anxiety, 29
Harvard Graduate School of Education, 15
Heckman, James, 16
helicopter parent, 1; as Shepherd, 136
herd mentality, 131
honesty, 35, 44, *172,* 173, 185
human development, 180
hyperachievement landscape, 181
hypercompetitive, 1, 2

identification, 50, 170–71
identifying triggers, 43–44, 46
identity: of Avoider, 109; separation and, 181; in values of values, 169
immigration, 81–82
imperfect decisions, 175–76, 178
impracticality, 138
indecision validity, 89
independence, 135, 136–37
individuality, 98; of Correctors, 152–53; of values of values, 169
internal conflict, 35–36
Iran emigration, 81–82

Jim. *See* Shepherds
judgment, 2, 45–46
Juliet example, 24–26
jumping to conclusions, 42–44, 141
junior year social support, 11–12

labeling: as cognitive distortion, 45–46, 47; by Crowd-Pleasers, 99; in Parenting Decision-Making Worksheet, 186; by Sculptor parents, 68; Sculptor parents and, 69
language processing disorder, 136
leave of absence, 138
Lee example, 24–26
Let's Make a Deal, 76